PROGRAM

ART & DESIGN

OF STUDY IN

A Handbook
for Teachers
Key Stage 3

GILLIAN WALLER

SIMON & SCHUSTER
EDUCATION

First published in 1992 in Great Britain by
Simon & Schuster Education,
Campus 400, Maylands Avenue,
Hemel Hemstead, Herts HP2 7EL

A catalogue for this book may be obtained from the British Library

ISBN 07501 02934

Designed and typeset by **AMR**

Printed in Hong Kong by Wing King Tong Co., Ltd.

ACKNOWLEDGEMENTS:

Thank you to my excellent colleagues at Fort Hill School for all their help and support,
especially Lesley Dixon and Mike Thomas who have both contributed to the material in this book.

Thank you to my family for their invaluable help in putting the book together,
especially my daughter Katherine.

A special thank you also to all the children, without whose work this book would not exist, and
to Simon Davies who worked with us on the animal project.

Marie Ahsun	Michael Daden	Chloé Hartnell	Rachel Morris	Dean Smith
Marie Ambler	Kevin Davis	Ingrid Hatt	Caroline McSweeney	Kerri Smith
Tracey Ambler	Ashley Devoy	Nicola Hayes	Stacey Neale	Melanie Smith
Ross Appleton	Paul Eastwood	Michael Henry	Gina Neville	Wayne Smith
Zoé Appleton	Craig Ellis	Gemma Horobin	Spencer Oliver	David Stent
Claire Arnett	Daniel Elsey	Julie Honour	Gillan Olney	Jo Swan
Craig Barnfield	Amanda Everard	Karen Honour	Anthony Page	Jamie Thompson
Roger Bateman	Sara Jane Ewins	Emma Hopkins	Lee Patching	Carl Thomas
Simon Black	Glenn Flowerday	Katie Hurry	Helen Patten	Sarah Turner
Corrie Blagdon	Kelli Ford	Emma Ironside	Louise Parnell	David Warren
Jimmy Bolger	Joanne Ford	David Isaacs	Lisa Penney	Tessa Wee
Phillip Bolger	Steven Ford	Faith Issacs	Robert Pollard	Jamie Welch
Eloise Bonsey	Lee Foster	Suzanne Lane	Vicki Rashbrook	Amy Wells
Chantal Brill	Simon Frazer	Mary Lee	Cindy Ralph	Karen West
Simon Brunger	Nicola Freeman	Thomas Lee	Paul Ralph	Sally Wheeler
Janette Burridge	Stuart Freeman	Sarah Martin	Neil Risley	Zoé White
Claire Carr	Sally French	Matthew Mason	Paul Rumsey	Jane White
Norma Casey	Maxime Gormley	Sarah Mecham	Jo Saunders	Joanne Whitmarsh
Corrina Champion	Stuart Gradd	Sharon Mecham	Louise Shorney	Julie Wilcock
Faye Churchley	Graham Hall	Joanne Mills	Luan Soper-Dyer	Laura Wilcock
Helen Churchley	Giles Hardy	Steven Mills	Gillian Spray	Jacob Williams
Andrew Clayton	Katie Harrison	Scott Minton	Jane Spray	Keith Young

CONTENTS

INTRODUCTION

This book is based very much on my own teaching and that of my colleagues, Lesley Dixon and Mike Thomas. All the illustrations are the work of children at Fort Hill School where I have worked for the last six years, but the ideas are based on the experience of over twenty years in education.

The art teacher has a special role in any school, one that is not always recognised by those in authority, but of which the art teacher is undoubtedly aware. It is the area of the curriculum that allows every child to communicate in a very personal way. Children are taught skills of observation, problem-solving and decision-making through shared visual experiences which enable personal visions to be externalised. It is a way of harnessing the creative facilities of the human spirit. The first role of the art teacher must always be to nurture confidence and enthusiasm for first-hand research and discovery. It seems to me that the National Curriculum sets out to encourage just that.

I have organised this Handbook into twenty-nine schemes of work which begin with my current Year Seven Syllabus and gradually become more difficult. However, there is no reason why the projects suggested at the beginning of the book could not be done at a number of different levels. The important thing is for the teacher to break the work down into simple steps for the children, so that by the time they reach Year Eleven they are able to work on individual projects with a fair degree of independence. This is not possible unless a good foundation has been laid.

As a young teacher I was most impressed by the notion of a 'self-fulfilling prophecy'. You tell the children they are good and they become good. What a beautifully simple idea! You may be sceptical, but I have found it to have a good deal of truth in it. Indiscriminately praising everything will not work, but selecting what is 'good' and highlighting that, will produce encouraging results.

During adolescence, children have very little confidence in their ability. They are continually comparing their efforts unfavourably with adult counterparts. The teacher has to produce strategies to deal with this perception of themselves. I hope this book addresses this problem with plenty of practical suggestions based on the National Curriculum Programmes of Study.

Gillian Waller, 1992

PART 1 SCHEMES OF WORK

1 SELF PORTRAIT

SESSION 1

Slide show

Starting Point

1A

Prepare a selection of slides containing a wide variety of portraits from different historical and cultural contexts. Include examples of early Christian, Egyptian and Oriental Art. Explore the notion that not all portraits are of an individual person, some are painted as symbols according to social and artistic rules and conventions. Egyptian Art, for example, had very strict laws. Men had to be painted with darker skins than women, their heads drawn in profile while their shoulders and chest had to be drawn from the front. The artist was not expected to produce an individual likeness. He had to follow the rule of including all the important details of anatomical structure in his work. The King was the person drawn larger than anyone else. How does this portrayal of a king compare with other cultures?

What did Henry VIII and Queen Elizabeth I want their portraits to say about them? How do their portraits differ from the paintings of the Royal Family today?

Contemporary portraits are fun to show because the children enjoy guessing who they are looking at by following visual clues. If possible, finish the slide show with a variety of self portraits by the same artist. (Van Gogh and Rembrandt provide numerous examples of these.)

Give the children small free-standing mirrors so that they can begin to make a study of themselves. Place great emphasis on looking before making any marks on paper. It is helpful to describe the biological details that should be observed: the structure of the eye; the shape of the tear duct, iris and lid, etc. Explain that drawing is done first in the brain by careful observation.

Before embarking on a study of the whole face, begin by getting the children to work on one small detail at a time, an eye, their nose, their lips, etc.

1C

1B

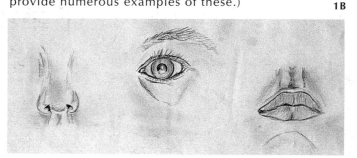

Homework 1

Suggest that the children make another study of their face at home. They can use paint or pastel if these things are available to them (Figures 1D and 1E).

1D   1E

SESSION 2

Drawing

Starting Point

Begin with a discussion. Ask the children which slides they remember from the last session. What did they remember about them, like about them? Review Homework 1 with the group. Can we recognise anyone? (They love playing a guessing game with their portraits.)

Give out the mirrors again and a sheet of A2 paper. Explain that the two pictures the children have done so far were their research. Now they are starting on their main picture. This portrait must tell us something about themselves in addition to their appearance. What are they interested in ? What do they do in their spare time? Their first decision is where to place themselves on the paper. Should they be sitting behind the windscreen of a car or an aeroplane? Should they be smiling from the screen of a computer or on the turntable of a record player? Once again the children draw themselves after careful observation in the mirror.

SESSION 3

Composition of picture

Starting Point

Ask the children to share the pictures and objects they have brought in from home. What would make the best arrangement of shapes?

After discussion, the children plan their pictures ready for painting next week.

1F   1G

Homework 2

Ask the children to draw and find pictures and objects to go into their pictures (Figures 1F and 1G).

Homework 3

Suggest that the children find interesting portraits from magazines and newspapers to glue into their sketch pads. Ask them why these were chosen.

S E S S I O N 4

Experimenting with painting techniques

Starting Point

Remind the children of the portraits they saw in the first session and discuss the different ways in which they were painted. Show them portraits painted in different styles, impressionists and Old Masters. Children need to experiment with painting on their preparatory drawings to discover which method of working they like best. Do they like watery thin paint or do they like to use it thick and show strong brush strokes like Van Gogh? Do they want to aim for realistic flesh tones or do they want to convey a mood by painting in blue tones like Picasso or bright, flat areas of colour like Matisse?

S E S S I O N S 5 & 6

Painting

Starting Point

Lead discussion of the discoveries made for Homework 4. After evaluating the success of various methods of painting, the children work on their main picture.

S E S S I O N 7

Evaluation

Starting Point

Follow with class discussion of their work. Children mount and display their main picture and the preparatory studies (examples of pictures are shown in Figures 1H and 1I).

Homework 4

Send the children to the library to find pictures of portraits by famous artists. Ask them to select one and write down the details about it: the name of the artist; who he was painting and when it was painted. Suggest they make a quick sketch and say what they like about it.

Evaluation

Ask the children to write an answer to the question... 'If I were going to work on this subject again, what would I do differently?' They should try to be as specific as possible, beginning with the skills they used and techniques they adopted, perhaps from other artists.

1H

1I

1J

Development

Helen painted her picture about herself putting great emphasis on the objects that are important to her. The portrait of herself has become the tiny silhouette figure in the centre of the picture surrounded by those objects that have entered her soul (Figure 1J.)

8

2 MASKS

SESSION 1

Research

2A

2B

2C

Starting Point

Show the children various examples of masks. Discuss the function of masks in different cultures: Greek, Oriental; African, etc. Ideally the children should visit a museum, such as the Pitt Rivers in Oxford, to draw some of the excellent examples of masks (Figure 2A).

Encourage them to find a variety of different types of masks to study, ensuring that they notice where they come from and what their function might be (Figures 2B and 2C).

Homework 1

Ask the children to go to the library and find further examples of masks and make studies of at least one of them in their sketch pads. See Figure 2D. (Make sure you warn the library first!)

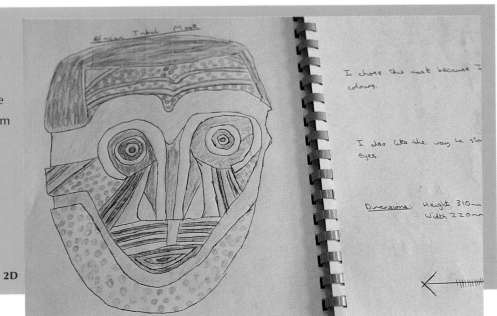

2D

SESSION 2

Designing

Give out some small free-standing mirrors. Ask the children how their faces change in shape when they smile; look angry; look sad, etc. Draw simple face shapes that express an emotion (Figure 2E).

The children select the expression they prefer and draw it to scale as a template for a mask.

Homework 2

Suggest that the children collect illustrations from comics, magazines and other media containing examples of faces expressing emotion and glue them into their sketch pads.

SESSIONS 3 & 4

Modelling

Starting Point

Discuss Homework 2. Do any of the children want to change their designs in response to their discoveries?

2E

Show them how a wet sponge will enable them to make the surface smooth before they work on textured patterns (Figure 2G).

2G

Encourage them to 'try out' textures on spare clay before they work on the mask itself (Figure 2H).

2H

Demonstrate how to make the mask curve by adding crushed newspaper underneath (Figure 2I).

2F

Show the class how to roll out a slab of clay and how to cut out a face shape. Get the children to feel their faces. Where are there hollows and raised areas? How can they create them in a flat sheet of clay? Show them how to make a sausage of clay and model it onto the mask to make the nose. Remind them that all the pieces of clay that are added need to be properly joined or they will fall off when the model dries (Figure 2F).

Help them to work on their own mask. Two sessions will probably be required to work on this. As long as the children wrap their work in polythene so that the air cannot get to it, it can safely be stored for up to a month to work on it again. Let it dry supported by the crushed newspaper.

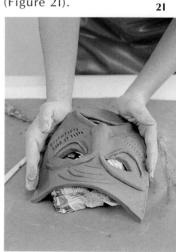

2I

SESSION 5

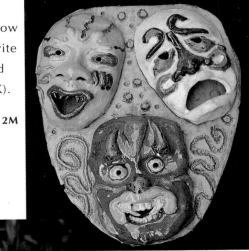

2K

2L

Glazing/ painting

Starting Point

Before glazing the work, spend a little time helping the children understand the changes that have taken place in the clay since it has been biscuit-fired.

Each child should make a careful drawing of the biscuit mask in their sketch pad so that they can record accurately the colours they have used (Figure 2J).

2J

It is a good idea to give out the glaze in clearly labelled pots so that everyone is able to work from those. (I usually give six different colours to each group of tables and then the children can share them.) Explain that the colours they are painting will only be apparent after a further firing.

Which colours would help to emphasise the mask's emotion? Show the children how to paint on the glaze. Children should write down details of the glazes they have used so they can assess their results (Figure 2K).

2M

Evaluation

Do the masks manage to express an emotion? Ask the children to compare the finished mask with their original plan. Have the glazes turned out as they expected? What could they have done to make the mask better (Figure 2L)?

Development

2N

Children could work on three masks designed to show a range of emotion as Joanne has done (Figure 2M).

Several different expressions could be incorporated into one free-standing head (details for construction are available in the unit on Portrait Heads). Figure 2N shows Spencer's example.

SESSIONS 1 & 2

Drawing from observation

Make arrangements to take the children out of the school grounds to make studies of local housing, or if that is not possible, the school site.

Starting Point

Ask the children to describe the buildings they pass on their way to school. What sort of buildings are they? Are they modern, high-rise, terraced, detached or Victorian? Discuss how local architecture has developed. How have people who live in terraced housing personalised their dwellings? In what type of building is the school situated? What were the architectural reasons for its structure? Ask the children to consider how their local environment has developed.

Explain that this lesson is designed to improve their powers of observation. They should notice the various textures of tiles, bricks, glass, etc. and

3A

they need to find a way to express this on paper. How can a pencil be used to express the shiny surface of glass or the texture of bushes (Figure 3A)?

While there, share a film between the class so that they can all photograph the view they were working from. This can be used during the next session if is is not possible to go out again (Figure 3B).

3B

Children who work quickly can add colour to their pictures. They may even take watercolours with them on their second visit so they can experience another medium (Figure 3C).

Development

Before going on to work in clay, the children could produce a painting based on their research as Rachel has done (Figure 3D).

3C

3D

Homework 1

Ask the children to draw the front of their house, not from memory, but by going out and looking at it.

SESSION 3

Experimenting

Starting Point

Show the children how to experiment to create different textures in clay.(It is useful to show examples of the little ceramic houses by South American potters so they can see how details like roof tiles may be created in clay.)

Let them experiment with rolled out slabs of clay to see how they might create the various textures of the buildings they have studied (Figure 3E). They should make a texture tile and put it out for firing so that it can be used to experiment with glazes.

Let them choose either their classwork or their homework and plan how they will translate it into a relief.

3E

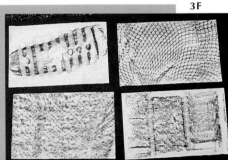

3F

Homework 2

Suggest the children make rubbings of different surfaces at home (Figure 3F).

Homework 3

Ask the children to make more texture rubbings. Explain that they will be using them in their next session.

SESSION 4

House tile

Starting Point

Show the children how to roll out slabs and translate their drawing into a textured surface on the clay.

Encourage them to experiment and discover their own way of doing things, using found objects as well as tools to create interesting surfaces. All separate pieces of clay need to be glued into place with slip (liquid clay made from the clay body) or they will fall off when the clay dries.

Make sure the tiles are laid out flat to dry. They can be stored on top of each other if they are kept on the wooden boards.

SESSION 5

Collage

Encourage the children to use the textured rubbings they made for Homework 3 to produce a texture collage based on their tile design.

When they have finished, they should test the glazes they are planning to use on their experimental tiles. Make sure they keep careful notes as this will enable them to identify what they have used (Figure 3G).

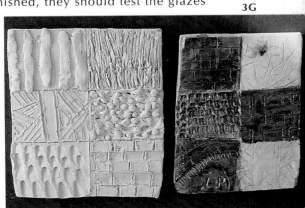

3G

SESSION 6

Glazing

Starting Point

As with the masks, children should draw their biscuit fired tiles into their books so they can carefully record which glazes they have used.

Evaluation

Have the children created interesting textural surfaces on their tiles? Have they used the glaze appropriately? (See Figures 3H and 3I).

Development

Instead of using textures, the tile could be worked with a sgraffito technique as Louise has done (Figure 3J). To do this, a sheet of red earthenware clay is rolled out and coated with white slip. When the tile is leather-hard, the design is drawn on and scratched away to reveal the red earthenware base. It can look very effective with a clear glaze. (See Part 3 Techniques).

3H

3I

Alternatively, the children could make three dimensional models of houses instead of tiles. This is done simply by rolling sufficient slabs of clay to form the walls and roof (usually six). Allow them to dry to become leather-hard. Then glue them together with soft clay (as described in Part 3 Techniques). The textures are then added once the model has been assembled.

3J

3K

SESSION 1

Drawing from observation

Starting Point

Begin with a discussion of what might be seen by looking out of a window. What might a prisoner see from his cell? A child in a war-torn street? What did Matisse and David Hockney see from their windows? Show the work of artists who have worked on this theme. What can the children see from their window? What do they wish they could see?

Arrange the seating so that all the children can see out of the windows. Tell them to begin by carefully drawing the window frame, putting in details such as window catches, etc. Then draw the things in front of the window as well as the things outside. This will create a feeling of perspective (Figure 4A).

4A

SESSION 2

Draughting the main picture

Starting Point

Begin with a discussion of the homework, showing examples of famous paintings to elicit the various ways in which the feeling of perspective is created.

The children should draw out their window on to A2 paper. They can decide on a view of their choice, but the frame must be convincing, even if, as Ashley has done (Figure 4D), they decide on a window in a car.

Homework 1

Children could draw the view from a window at home. Again they need to show the frame and anything in front of the window, such as curtains (Figures 4B and 4C).

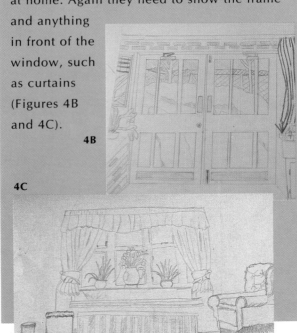

4B

4C

4D

The picture can be purely realistic, an accurate description of what they can see, like Robert's (Figure 4E), or it may be imaginative like Philip's (Figure 4F) – what they would love to see, or what they would hate.

Homework 2

Ask the children to find pictures and make drawings of things to include in their work.

SESSIONS 3 & 4

Painting

Starting Point

Explain that when they are painting their pictures they must use colour to make a contrast between the things inside and outside. They may decide to make everything inside the room dark and gloomy and everything outside bright and colourful, or the reverse. Limit them to one colour, plus black for the gloomy aspect, and this should be painted first.

They need to get into the habit of trying out colours and effects on 'study sheets' before working directly on their main pictures. Maxine spent a long time planning out her techniques before deciding on her final picture. In fact, she decided not to paint the interior of her window but to shade it with pencil to produce a picture with a strong contrast (Figures 4G and 4H).

Evaluation

Have the children succeeded in creating a feeling of perspective in their pictures? Have they made a contrast in mood between the interior and exterior of their rooms?

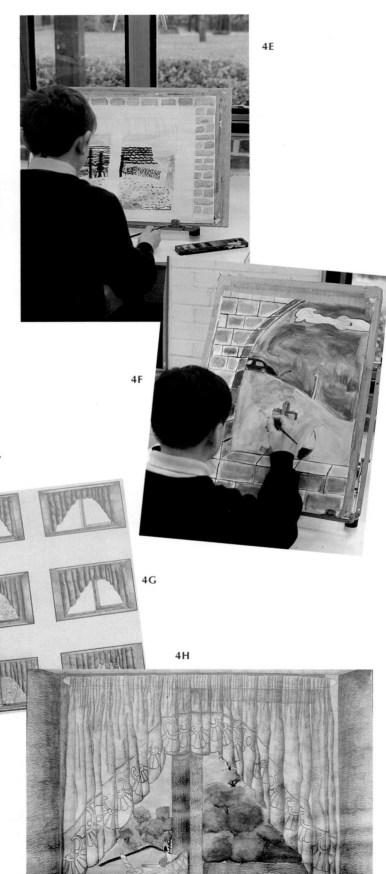

4E

4F

4G

4H

16

Development

Clay models

The windows could be translated into a clay model. They look very effective with a mirror tile inserted behind the frame. This is glued into place after firing (Figure 4I).

4I

Wood and plastic model

Kevin worked on a model of a window frame using wood and plastic. Here the window has been broken as the flower is transformed into a fish (Figure 4J).

4J

5 PLANT STUDIES

SESSION 1

Drawing from observation

Starting Point

Arrange a large variety of plants in the centre of the room so the children can see them clearly. A circular arrangement usually works well (Figure 5A).

Children should observe the plants and draw them as carefully as possible, leaving out the plant pots, concentrating on the different leaf shapes. It is best to work on good cartridge paper which is stretched on to boards for watercolour painting. (See Part 3 Techniques.)

5A

Homework 1

Ask the children to find examples of wrapping paper, wall paper, printed cloth, etc. which are based on leaf designs. These should be glued into sketch pads or sketched and brought to the next session. The children should write brief notes to say what they like about them (Figure 5B).

5B

SESSION 2

Painting

Starting Point

Show the children examples of artists who have painted plants using watercolour techniques. (The work of Sarah Bibra would provide a contemporary example, while Cozens, Girtin, Cotman and Turner are the greatest practitioners of ths art.) Point out that watercolour works by building up different strengths of colour by varying the amount of water you use.

Give them 'testing papers' to experiment with mixing different strengths of colour before they paint on their main picture.

The children then paint leaf-shape pictures using paint in different strengths in response to the subtle hues of the leaves (Figure 5C).

5C

Examples of the children's paintings are shown in Figures 5D, 5E and 5F.

Homework 2

Suggest that the children make a drawing of plants at home, either inside or outside. Ask them why they chose the plants they drew.

5D

5E

5F

5G

5H

SESSION 3

Plate design

Starting Point

Discuss a variety of plates that have leaf designs as decoration. (For example the contemporary work of Alan Caiger-Smith and David Eeles who use brushwork, or Mary Wondrausch who uses a sgraffito technique.) Give out black sugar paper and white pencils and tell the children to draw a large circle to represent a plate. They must select the best part of their picture and draw it out onto their plate. Tracing paper may be used to select their best leaf shapes.

They should now use white paint either to paint the leaves or to paint the background. This will produce a fairly abstract design (Figures 5G and 5H).

Homework 3

Ask the children to find a decorated plate or dish at home and draw its design in their sketch pad.

Evaluation

Do the designs fit into the plate shape well?

SESSION 4

Making dishes

Starting Point

Demonstrate how to make a simple plate using a dish mould (Figure 5I and see Part 3 Techniques). If dish moulds are not available, a tile may be decorated instead, or a china plate may be used as long as it is lined with an absorbent surface, such as a paper towel or newspaper.

5I

Children make their own dishes either in red or grey clay. If they are working in red clay, they can paint their plates with white slip. If they are using grey clay, they should paint them with a reactive slip as in Figure 5J. (See Part 3 Techniques.) The dishes must now be left to dry until they are leather-hard.

5J

Homework 4

In their sketch pads, they could use simple diagrams to describe the process of making the dish.

SESSION 5

Sgraffito decoration

Starting Point

Explain that we have now created a dish which has a thin coating of white over a dark-coloured body. If we scratch a line through the white coating, the colour underneath will show through.

Show the children how to draw out their design onto the plate using a pencil (Figure 5K) and then how to scratch out the area that was black on their original design (Figure 5L).

5K

5L

End the lesson by showing photographs of the wonderful ceramics of Ancient Greece where this method of working was used to illustrate stories about the Gods.

Homework 5

Suggest that the children go to the library and draw the decoration used by some of the potters of Ancient Greece. Say why they like them.

S E S S I O N 6

Glazing

Starting Point

Plates are finished by giving them a transparent glaze if you have been using red clay, or a dolomite glaze if you've been using grey clay and reactive slip (Figures 5M and 5N). See Part 3 Techniques for glazing.

5M

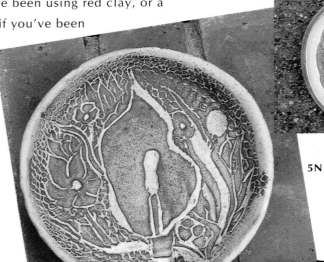

5N

Final outcomes are shown in Figures 5O and 5P.

5O

5P

Homework 6

Final evaluation

Have the children realised their designs well? Suggest that they ask parents and friends to comment on their plates.

SESSIONS 1 & 2

Drawing from observation

Starting Point

The children observe plants as described for the previous scheme of work. They should be encouraged to use a range of media: oil pastels and dry pastels and paint thickened with PVA medium (Figure 6A). If they work with white paint on black paper, it is easy to abstract a design (Figure 6B).

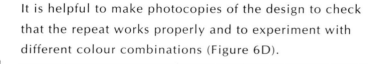

6A

6B

SESSION 3

Designing

Starting Point

Show the children examples of good fabric design (William Morris is an excellent example). Ask them to identify the device that has been used to enable the print to repeat without showing the join. Children select their best leaf shapes and simplify them into bold simple shapes. See Figure 6C.

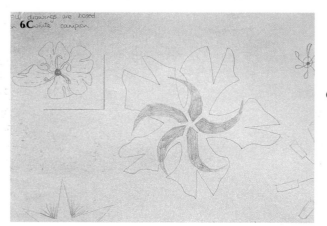

6C

They should use tracing paper to work out a design that will repeat. The use of a stem that begins and ends the same distance from the edge of the paper is very helpful. (See Part 3 Techniques).

It is helpful to make photocopies of the design to check that the repeat works properly and to experiment with different colour combinations (Figure 6D).

Homework 1

The children are asked to find examples of printed cloth and wallpaper at home and copy the design to illustrate the way it has been planned to repeat.

Evaluation

How successful have they been in planning their repeat?

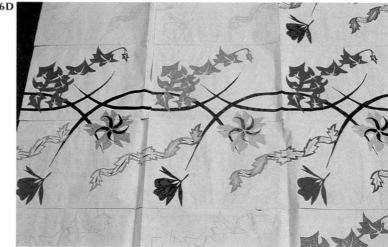

6D

SESSION 4

Stencils

Starting Point

Explain to the children that each colour needs to be printed separately in a silk-screen print. They need to decide how many colours they are going to use and plan their stencil accordingly.

Figures 6E, 6F and 6G show the three separate stencils that Gill had to use in order to produce her print.

Very good results can be achieved with only one colour if it is planned carefully. Jane's design, shown in Figures 6H and 6I, is a good example.

6E

6F

6G

6H

6I

Paper stencils are cut using a craft knife (see Part 3 Techniques) and children are asked to bring in old pillow cases, sheets and table cloths ready to print in the next session.

SESSION 5

Printing

See Part 3 Techniques for step-by-step details of the process.

Evaluation

Have the children been successful in producing a print? Does it repeat well? Is the repeat very obvious or do you have to look to find it? Has it been worked in more than one colour? Have the colours been registered well?

23

SESSION 1

Drawing from observation

Starting Point

Begin by asking the children to look down at their feet. Have they ever considered what the world looks like to them?

Arrange shoes on the table stuffed with newspaper so that they appear to be walking. (Children may use their own shoes or ones provided by the teacher.) It is more interesting to have a wide variety of footwear (Figures 7A and 7B).

Give the class A2 paper and tell them to draw the shoes as carefully as they can, as though they were about to walk off the table.

Where are these feet walking? Are they walking through the town or countryside, or dancing at a party? Try to tell a story by concentrating on a foot's eye view of the world.

7B

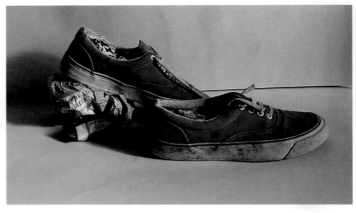

SESSION 2

Developing the picture

Starting Point

Begin the session by looking at famous paintings to see how artists go about building a feeling of perspective in their pictures. Get the class to explain that the objects in the front are drawn to a larger scale to those in the background and that the colours in the front are bright while those in the distance are subdued. Encourage the children to develop their pictures around their initial studies. Where possible they should draw from real objects in the classroom... crisp packets, plants, chair legs, etc.

Homework 2

Suggest that the children make a careful study of something close to the ground that they normally do not notice. They should try to choose something that would be useful to include in a picture. (Figures 7C and 7D)

7C

7A

Homework 1

Ask the children to use their sketch pads to work out the story the feet can tell.

7D

SESSIONS 3, 4 & 5

Adding colour

Starting Point

Review Homework 2 together. Who has discovered something no one else has considered?

Discuss how colour may be added to the pictures. Children could use watercolour paint, thick squeezy bottle paint, oil pastel, dry pastel or pen and ink. They should experiment with the media on 'practice papers' before working on the main piece.

Figures 7E, 7F and 7G show examples of different outcomes by Karen, Luan and Andrew.

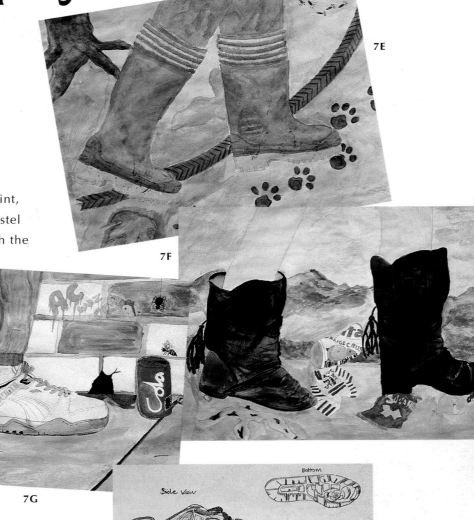

7E

7F

7G

7H

Evaluation

Have the children made good use of their original studies? Have they managed to create a feeling of perspective in their picture? Have they been sensitive in their use of paint?

SESSION 6

Modelling shoes: drawing from observation

Starting Point

Children should take off one shoe and place it in front of them on the table so they can see it clearly.

Give out A3 paper and ask them to draw their shoe from at least three different viewpoints, paying particular attention to details of stitching, fastenings, etc. (Figure 7H).

Homework 3

Children make studies of different types of shoes at home.

SESSION 7

Paper modelling

Starting Point

Give the children rough paper, scissors and glue and ask them to work out how to make their shoe out of paper. Suggest that if they copy the shapes of the leather pieces it should be easy (Figure 7I).

SESSION 8

Constructing in clay

Starting Point

Explain to the children that they are now going to use clay instead of paper and that they can use the paper shoe they made last week as a paper pattern to lay on the rolled-out clay. The clay is much easier to work with than the paper because it will stretch and hold its shape (Figure 7J).

SESSIONS 9 & 10

Modelling

Starting Point

Children work on their clay shoes and add details to make the shoe tell a story. Is there a foot in the shoe?

Maybe the wheel of a shopping trolley is squashing someone's toe? Perhaps someone is about to slip on a banana skin, or perhaps the shoe is ready to be polished? Children should work on their model to make it unique.

7K, 7L and 7M are examples of different outcomes.

SESSION 11

Glazing

Starting Point

Glazing of biscuit-fired work is the aim of this session. Children should make notes of the glazes they use so they can evaluate their results.

Evaluation

Have the children made a successful model? Have they managed to use the clay well? Have they included detailed modelling of texture (such as stitching and fastenings, etc.)? Have they used the model to express an idea?

Development

Graham used shoe shapes to construct a monument based on Stonehenge (Figure 7N).

26

8 ANIMAL STUDIES: MODELLING

SESSION 1

Researching

Starting Point

Ideally the starting point for this work should be studies of living creatures, perhaps a visit to a farm, zoo or park. Alternatively, children could bring in their hamsters, goldfish or docile dogs (be brave!). Failing this, children could make studies from photographs, drawing animals from more than one viewpoint so that they consider how they look as three dimensional forms.

Encourage children to experiment with different media such as pen and ink, oil pastel and charcoal to create the texture of fur or feathers, etc. (Figures 8A and 8B).

8A

8B

SESSIONS 2 & 3

Modelling

Starting Point

Show the work of artists and craftspeople who have captured the spirit of individual creatures. (Examples include Brancussi's bird, fish or seal, the anthropomorphic vessels of pre-Colombian ceramics or the clay models of Tessa Fuchs.)

Demonstrate how to make a hollow shape by rolling out a slab of clay and then wrapping it around a ball of newspaper. This gives the children a strong form that can be altered into the animal of their choice. The newspaper will burn away during firing, so they must remember to make a small hole to allow steam to escape in the kiln. Now they need to add extra clay to make a convincing animal form. (They must remember not to use clay that is too thick. If it is thicker than their thumb it is likely to break during firing.) Encourage them to experiment in creating textural details. (Figures 8C, 8D and 8E show the main steps.)

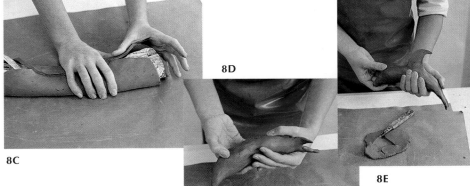

8D

8C

8E

Homework 1

Ask the children to find pictures and make studies of animals at home.

Homework 2

Ask the children to find pictures of animal models. What are they made of? Brass, porcelain, wood? Have these materials been used well to express the shape of the animal?

SESSION 4

Glazing

Starting Point

Children paint glaze onto their biscuit-fired models, keeping notes in their sketch pad that will enable them to identify the glazes they have used. Figures 8F, 8G, 8H, 8I and 8J are examples of outcomes.

Evaluation

Has the child managed to convey the spirit of the animal he or she was studying? Is the model three dimensional, or has it really only been considered from one viewpoint?

8F

8G

8H

8I

8J

SESSION 1

Researching

Starting Point

Introduce the class to the work of the Constructivists, Naum Gabo and Antoine Pevsner, so they can appreciate the light airy qualities of work when space is dissected by flat planes.

Ideally this work should be initiated by a visit to a bird sanctuary or by watching a video of birds in flight. Failing this the children will have to work from photographs. They should begin by studying the shape of birds' wings when they are flying. Encourage them to select one type of bird and concentrate on the way it spreads its wings (Figure 9A).

9A

SESSION 2

Designing

The children continue with the drawing they began last week, simplifying the form of the bird they have chosen so that they capture the essence of its movement.

SESSION 3

Constructing

9B

Show the children how to make a three-dimensional model of a bird using card. They need to cut out the shape of the wings from one piece and the body from another. This will require them to simplify the shape to a bold form. The wings and body are then stapled or glued together (Figure 9B).

SESSION 4

Refining

9C

The card birds can be finished by giving them a spray of black paint and mounting them onto wood, or they could be used as a template to be cut out of sheet steel and riveted together before spraying and mounting (Figures 9C, 9D and 9E).

Evaluation

9D

Has the child produced a construction based on his or her original drawings? Has it captured the spirit of the bird in flight?

9E

29

SESSION 1

Researching

Starting Point

Show pictures of animals as they are depicted in different cultures. Ideally a visit to a museum would be the most inspiring, (e.g. aboriginal bark paintings; Chinese animal masks; Peruvian ceramics; as well as batik from Indonesia, etc.). Ask the children to carefully draw the ones they like the best and to say what they like about them.

Ask them to select which of their studies they like the best and to draw it out with good clear outlines so that it fills an A4 sheet (Figure 10A).

They need to colour it in with only two colours: one light and the other fairly dark.

10A

Homework 1

Suggest that the children try to find examples of animal designs on fabrics, wallpaper, wrapping paper, etc.

SESSION 2

Waxing

10B

Preparation

Before the lesson begins, have the wax melted and put it safely out of the way until you are ready to use it. The wax needs to be heated until a little hazy blue smoke appears.

Starting Point

Show the children examples of batik, preferably from Indonesia. Use photographs if no actual designs are available.

Give out fabric squares to every child, approximately 30 cm each. (I rely on old sheets from jumble sales.) Explain that they need to draw out their design very clearly in pencil before they begin.

Show them how to paint their design using hot wax to cover the areas they want to remain white. If they are using a tjanting for the first time, tell them to scribble with it on a piece of scrap paper to get the feel of it. The wax runs out of the nozzle very quickly and may form a blob. If that happens, advise them just to continue and make the blob part of their design. Old paintbrushes can be used, but they are never quite the same to paint with!

Make sure all the children are clear about how to use the wax safely before they begin (Figure 10B).

When they have finished waxing, put all the fabric into the light-coloured dye and leave for the recommended time to take on the colour. Let all the fabric dry before the next session.

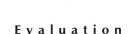
10C

10D

SESSION 3

Adding second colour

Starting Point

Show the children how to paint the wax on again so that the areas they want to remain the first colour are covered (Figure 10C). Again, put all the fabric into the dye and allow it to dry (Figure 10D).

SESSION 4

Evaluating

Starting Point

Iron out the wax to see the final results (Figures 10E and 10F).

10E

10F

Evaluation

Was the design appropriate for this type of work? Was the child able to plan the stages and adapt her or his design to take into account the nature of the medium? Was the end result a success?

SESSION 1

Researching

Starting Point

Again this work is best based on a museum visit. Somewhere such as the British Museum or the Victoria and Albert Museum in London or the Pitt Rivers Museum in Oxford. The children need to be familiar with the anthropomorphic forms of Peruvian and Medieval pottery. They should begin the first session by making studies of these to see how other cultures have used animal forms in the moulding of their pots. A number of contemporary potters also work on this theme (Rosemary Wren).

Homework 1

Ask the children to work out a design for a pot based on an animal form.

SESSIONS 2 & 3

Coiling

Starting Point

Show the children how to make a coil pot (see Part 3 Techniques). They need to roll out the clay for the base and then build the walls by joining the coils of clay together. Explain that you want them to build the walls firmly

11A

11B

together and work on the basic shape before they put on any fine detail. They will probably need one whole session working on the basic shape and a following session to put on details of eyes, scales and wings.

It will, also, be easier for them if they work with thick coils (See Figure 11A, 11B and 11C).

11C

Homework 2

Challenge the children to find examples of contemporary pottery based on animal forms (such as teapots based on cats; egg containers shaped like chickens, etc.).

SESSION 4

Glazing

Starting Point

The children should try to find the appropriate finish for their pots, making careful notes of the colours they have used so they can evaluate their results.

Examples of the children's work are shown in Figures 11D, 11E and 11F.

11D

11E

Evaluation

Did the child manage to include characteristics of an animal in his design? Were they appropriate to this medium?

11F

SESSION 1

Researching

Starting Point

This work is best done after a visit to a museum, but it can be done by working from photographs of animal designs. Aboriginal bark paintings, primitive pottery and tomb painting can give the children a sense of design that they may not discover simply by looking at photographs of animals.

Help the children to work out a design that can be expressed in terms to texture a tile. They need to emphasise elements of line and pattern so they will create an interesting surface.

Homework 1

Suggest library research for this subject.

SESSION 2

Modelling

Starting Point

Show the children how to roll out the clay and make a wall all around the perimeter to hold in the plaster. Explain they are using the clay to make a mould for Plaster of Paris.

When they are sure the construction is sound, they may draw out their animal design so that it will create interesting textures. They should experiment with pressing-in tools and a variety of found objects (combs, nuts and bolts, pencil points, etc.) to add to the effect (Figure 12A).

12A

12B

When they are happy with their designs, mix up the Plaster of Paris and pour it into the moulds to set (Figure 12B). This needs to be left for at least two or three hours. It is very important that the children write their names on the top of the plaster before the end of this session so that each child can easily identify his or her work.

Ideally the plaster moulds should be wrapped in a polythene bag, to prevent the clay from drying out, and left until the next session.

Homework 2

The children should plan how they will paint their tiles next session.

SESSION 3

Painting

Starting Point

Show the children how to remove the clay by carefully easing it away from the plaster (Figure 12C).

Give out paint or coloured ink so the children can add colour.

Figure 12D shows examples of the children's finished tiles.

12C

12D

Evaluation

Were the children able to translate their drawings into a textural surface? Did they understand the nature of working on a negative mould? Were the textures in keeping with their design? Did they manage to paint it appropriately?

13 ANIMAL STUDIES: DECORATED DISHES

SESSION 1

Researching

Starting Point

Begin by getting the children to look at the way primitive, Oriental and contemporary potters have used animal designs on their work. Encourage the children to work out their own design based on an animal motif that could go onto a plate.

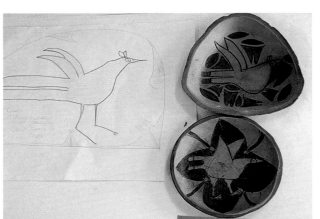

13A

Homework 1

The children should find examples of designs based on animal forms from the things they have at home, or they may find examples in magazines, the library, etc.

SESSION 2

Making press mould dishes

Starting Point

Demonstrate how to make terracotta dishes using a mould as described in Part 3 Techniques. Coat them with slip and allow them to become leather-hard. (Do not allow them to dry because the dust is harmful if you attempt sgraffito on dry ware.)

Once the dishes are made, the children should modify their designs to produce an image that is in sympathy with the shape of their plate.

SESSION 3

Sgraffito

Starting Point

Show the children how to draw out their design on a plate and how to scratch away the top layer of slip to reveal the red earthenware body (refer to 5 Plant Studies).

Figure 13A shows how two children used the same starting point to produce different designs. Figure 13B shows a group of plates, produced by the class, waiting for biscuit-firing.

13B

SESSION 4

Glazing

Glaze the biscuit-fired dishes with a transparent glaze.

Evaluation

Were the childen able to develop their designs so they used the plate shape efficiently? Were they able to master the sgraffito technique so there was a balance between the two coloured clays?

SESSION 1

Drawing from observation

Starting Point

In the centre of the room set up a large dustbin turned on its side with all kinds of rubbish spilling out of it (Figure 14A). Arrange the children so they can all see it easily.

Ask the children what they think of our 'throw away society'. What do they think of the way we look after our planet?

Explain to them that they are going to begin a unit of work on conservation of the environment. They will begin by making studies of the rubbish falling out of the bin. They need be sure to draw the objects as they are, one on top of another, not as separate shapes (Figure 14B).

Homework 1

In their sketch pads, the children work out ideas for a picture which will make people think about caring for our planet. Any aspect of conservation may be chosen, but the final picture must be eye-catching.

SESSION 2

Designing

Starting Point

Review Homework 1 and discuss the ideas. Look at posters published by Greenpeace and other environmentally-aware groups. Examine the work of The Expressionists and others who have worked on a similar theme. What makes them effective? Suggest that they now combine their ideas for an eye-catching poster with their studies of rubbish.

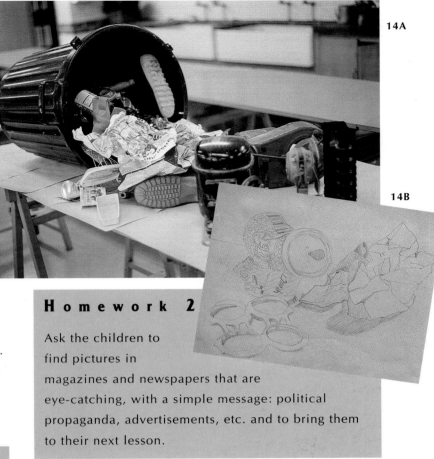

14A

14B

Homework 2

Ask the children to find pictures in magazines and newspapers that are eye-catching, with a simple message: political propaganda, advertisements, etc. and to bring them to their next lesson.

SESSIONS 3 & 4

Developing the final work

Starting Point

Pupils develop their own poster, painting or model which will make us all think a little more carefully about the way we look after our planet.

14C

Sally used the dustbin as the centre-piece in a picture designed to show the health risks as associated with rubbish (Figure 14C).

Stuart included his dustbin into the city skyline (Figure 14D).

14D

14E

14F

Just a walk in the park...

Gillian and Claire used the studies they made of packaging to show how our parkland and animal habitats are spoiled by litter (Figures 14E and 14F).

Marie produced two pictures; one of the countryside unspoiled, the other of the same area destroyed by pollution (Figures 14G and 14H).

14G

14H

Helen produced a painting to show how she was unable to sleep because of the worries that polluted her mind (Figure 14L).

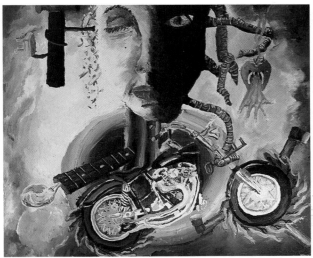

14I

14L

Steven saw a world where the whale was stranded in the desert and only sand came from the taps (Figure 14I).

Corrina went on to develop a picture, about the sufferings of people involved in war, into a silk-screen print (Figures 14M and 14N).

Roger and Paul made models of rubbish, Paul showing a dead mouse poisoned by its contents (Figures 14J and 14K).

14M

14J

14K

14N

Evaluation

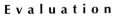

Did the children manage to produce work that conveyed a message? How successful were they in forcing the onlooker to think about the environment? Were they able to show a development of their ideas?

15 LIGHT

SESSION 1

Investigating

Starting Point

Set up a large group of objects in the centre of the room. (Preferably they should be predominantly white set against white sheets.) The local refuse tip is a great source for these objects. Show slides of paintings where colour has been used to create a mood. Examples of Monet's grainstacks are excellent for this because the subject is constant, but different lighting transforms them. Examples of Picasso's blue period are also useful, as too are William Blake's watercolours because of his limited palette.

At the end of the slide show, project three or four coloured gels onto the objects and discuss the moods they create.

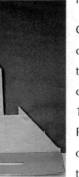

15A

Children can work from the central display or they can have their own display if you give out cardboard box corners (Figure 15A) and squares of white cloth. Pairs of children can create their own still-life group selecting from the central display (Figure 15B).

They need to draw their objects carefully, but should not attempt any shading. Ideally they should stretch their paper onto their drawing boards at the end of the session.

15B

Homework 1

Suggest that the children make notes on the changing colours of the sky during one day.

SESSIONS 2 & 3

Painting

Starting Point

Show the children how to use thin washes of paint to create tone. Allow them to use black and one other colour only to paint their pictures. White is created by leaving the white of the paper showing. The choice of the other colour is up to them. They can decide on the mood for their picture. Figures 15C, 15D and 15E are examples of pupils' work.

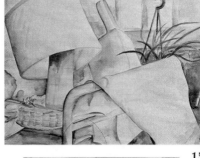

15

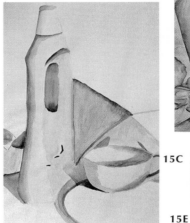

15C

15E

Homework 2

Ask the children to make a study of a group of objects from home. Use only a pencil for shading (Figure 15F).

15F

SESSION 4

Pastel work

Starting Point

Before the lesson, arrange plants and objects in front of the classroom windows. The children are going to draw negative shapes. Turn off the lights in the room and arrange the children so that they can see out of the windows. Give out black sugar paper and white chalk, asking them to draw the shape of the white light coming from the windows. Where there are objects in front of the window they should leave the paper black.

Figures 15G and 15H are examples of pupils' work.

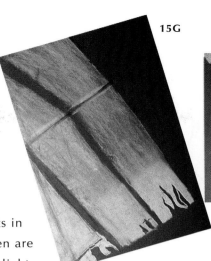

15G

15H

Homework 3

Suggest that the children make a study of someone seated at home. (People usually sit still in front of the television!)

SESSION 5

Drawing

Starting Point

Arrange the room so that the children can see a model occupying a comfortable seat in the centre of the room. Set up a bright light so that it casts strong shadows across the model. Turn out the class lights and black out the windows (Figure 15I).

15I

Give out black sugar paper and white pencils. The children should forget that they are drawing a person and concentrate only on shading areas of light. They can start anywhere on the figure: the sleeve; foot; leg, etc. and follow the lines of light. They will be pleased to discover a figure appear as in Figure 15J.

15J

SESSION 6

Drawing

15K

Starting Point

Repeat the same exercise but this time give out a mid-tone coloured paper and black pencils as well as the white ones. This will enable the children to draw in the heaviest shadow as well as the light. Figure 15K is an example of a successful result.

Homework 4

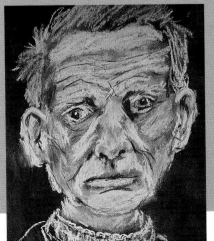

Ask the children to make a study of someone's face using pastel on a dark paper (Figure 15L).

15L

39

SESSION 7

15M

Development into new media

PAINTED OUTCOMES

The children can use the studies they have made for this unit to produce a 'mood' picture. Good examples are Rachel's 'Streets of London' (Figure 15M) or Lisa's 'Nightmare' (Figure 15N).

15N

PRINTED OUTCOMES

The figure studies lend themselves to be translated directly as a lino print. The example here is by Lisa (Figures 15O and 15P).

15O

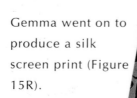

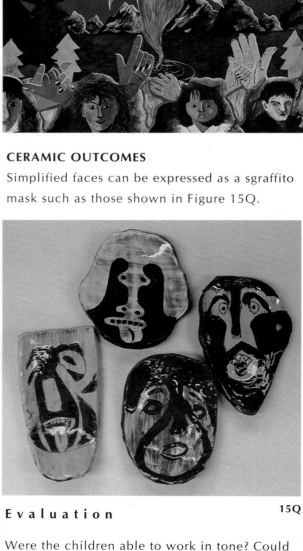

15P

CERAMIC OUTCOMES

Simplified faces can be expressed as a sgraffito mask such as those shown in Figure 15Q.

Gemma went on to produce a silk screen print (Figure 15R).

15R

Evaluation

15Q

Were the children able to work in tone? Could they appreciate light and shadow? Were they able to use the media (watercolour, chalk, pastel, etc.) effectively? Were they able to develop their own work?

16 REFLECTIONS

SESSION 1

Drawing from observation

Starting Point

Gather together a large range of shiny objects: light bulbs, kettles, tea pots, spoons, bath taps, wine bottles, etc. and ask the children to choose three of different sizes and shapes to work from (Figures 16A and 16B).

16A

16B

Ask the children to describe all the things they can see in their objects. How are they distorted when they look at their reflection?

Suggest that the class are to begin drawing, but they should make no attempt at shading. They must concentrate only on linear shapes. They need to draw the shape of the white light as they see it reflected in the object, and they should draw the shape of the heaviest shadow. They are thus

Homework 1

Ask the children to discover the reflections around them which they normally do not notice: shop windows; wheel hubs; car bonnets, for example. They could make a study of one in their sketch pads and write a list of any interesting or memorable ones (Figure 16C).

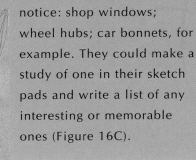
16C

SESSIONS 2 & 3

Working with ink

Starting Point

Discuss Homework 1 and share discoveries.

16D

Give out black ink, and dip pens. Show the children how to use the pens to outline their drawing.

Distribute thin paint brushes to paint black ink in the areas of deepest shadow. The children should take care not to lose the hard black line and they need to paint the black ink on evenly so that it is flat.

The children should choose a coloured ink to colour in the rest of their objects, but they must be very careful to keep the areas of white light free from ink. They must stand out as white (Figure 16D).

16E

Figures 16E and 16F are examples of children's work.

16F

Homework 2

The children are asked to find their own reflected image to work on in the next lesson.

SESSION 4

Development

Starting Point

Show examples of the work of artists on the subject of reflections.(For example the 'Bar at the Folies-Bergere' by Manet; the Arnolfini Marriage Portrait from the National Gallery and how it influenced Ford Maddox-Brown in 'Take your Son, Sir'.)

Discuss how the reflection changes our view of the picture by offering us another perspective.

Review Homework 2 and discuss how individuals might develop their own work. Figures 16G to 16P are examples of different types of children's work.

Gina's silk-screen print is based on reflections in skyscrapers. (Figures 16G and 16H).

Lisa's silk-screen print is based on bottles (Figures 16I, 16J and 16K).

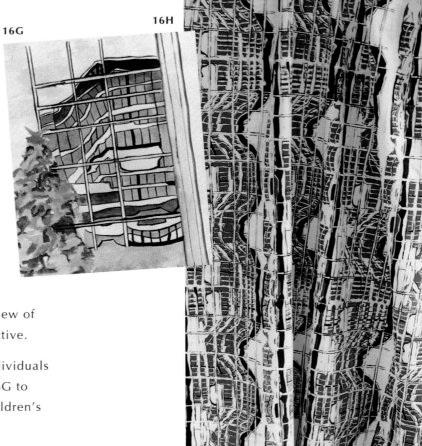

16G

16H

16J

16I

16K

Lee's silk-screen print is based on a still-life group (Figures 16L and 16M).

16L

16M

Joanne's painting is based on reflections in a mirror (Figure 16N).

16N

Lee has produced a shaded study of stylised reflections (Figure 16O).

16O

Steven's self portrait is in a shattered mirror (Figure 16P).

16P

Evaluation

Were the children able to abstract light and shadow into flat areas of colour? Were they able to use the ink appropriately? Were they able to develop work of their own effectively?

SESSION 1

Painting experiments

Starting Point

Begin by discussing the nature of water. How have artists chosen to depict it in paint? Give all the class a

17A

postcard or photograph of a famous painting that has water and ask the children to try to copy the artist's use of paint. (David Hockney, Turner and the Impressionists are excellent to work from.)

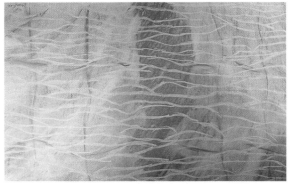
17B

The children enlarge details of water, working directly with paint (Figures 17A and 17B).

Homework 1

Ask the children to collect pictures of water. These can be pictures from magazines and newspapers as well as their own photographs.

SESSION 2

Drawing from observation

Ideally this should be a visit, either to a local duck pond, river or swimming pool. (I usually go to the local swimming pool because this visit does not depend on good weather.)

Starting Point

Show examples of David Hockney's swimming pools to the class. They are going to concentrate on the patterns of light reflected on water in a similar way to him. The subject of their picture is the water, not the people in it or the surrounding view.

Give the children drawing boards to work on and a box of dry pastels. These enable a fairly quick response. They are to look carefully at the water surface and then recreate that (Figure 17C).

17C

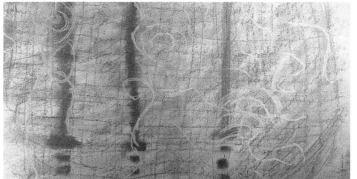
17D

Figures 17D and 17E are examples of children's studies from the pool. At the end of the session, enable them to take a photograph of the area they were studying so that they have this available for further research. (The class can share one film between them.)

17E

Homework 2

Ask the children to continue to collect photographic material based on water reflections. These should be brought to the next session.

S E S S I O N 3

Development

Children continue to develop pictures based on their visit, working with paint and using the photographs as an additional resource.

Figures 17F, 17G and 17H are examples of pupils' paintings.

17F

17G

17H

17I

17J

S E S S I O N 4

Abstracting a design

Starting Point

Review all the gathered material as a class and then ask each individual to mount up all the research they have gathered so far. (Their initial painting, the waterside research and their photographs as in Figure 17I).

Is there one of these that has a very clear pattern that could be developed? Encourage the children to select the one they like best and enlarge it, concentrating on the pattern of ripples, or reflections.

Homework 3

The children need to think of a way to develop water studies into a new medium. Various media can be used: e.g. collage, painting, silk-screen print or ceramics. They should draw out possible development plans in a sketch book.

S E S S I O N 5

Developing abstractions

17K

Starting Point

The development of ideas into individual projects needs individual discussion between the teacher and each pupil, followed by experimentation to develop appropriate processes and techniques.

Figures 17J to 17Q are examples from pupils.

Joanne's silk-screen print is based on her painting of ripples (Figures 17J and 17K).

17L

Faith's ceramic tile is based on her observations. (Figures 17L, 17M and 17N).

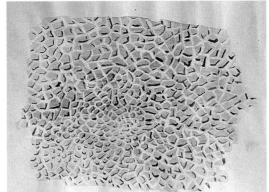

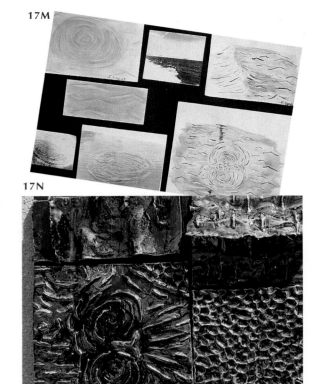

17M

17N

Gemma's pots are decorated with water ripples (Figure 17O).

17O

David's large abstract painting includes convincing water ripples (Figure 17Q).

17Q

Norma has made a wave study (Figure 17P).

17P

Evaluation

Were the children able to copy painting techniques from famous artists? Were they able to record the surface of water from direct observation? Were they able to develop their own work from their studies?

18 HANDS

SESSION 1

Drawing from observation

Starting Point

Ask the children to study their hands. What do their fingers look like? What sort of lines can they see on their palm?

Give out A3 paper and tell them to make four different studies of their hands. They can begin by simply enlarging their thumb and drawing that as accurately as possible, or enlarging the details on their palm, before embarking on a study of the whole hand. If children draw around their fingers on their first attempt, that won't matter as long as they draw in the details of knuckles and veins from observation and then draw the other three studies free-hand. They often need to do something like that to gain confidence (Figure 18A).

18A

End the lesson by reviewing the children's achievements, and discussing the symbolic and expressive nature of hand movements.

Homework 1

Ask the children to make a study of their hand, holding an object or making a symbolic gesture (not a rude one) as in Figure 18B.

18B

SESSIONS 2 & 3

Modelling

Session 1 work could now be developed into an expressive picture using the hand studies as in the example by Lisa (shown in Figure 18C).

An alternative is to make it into a ceramic sculpture.

18C

Starting Point

Gather the children around your table and review their Homework 1 with them. Show the children photographs of expressive modelling of hands by Rodin and Michaelangelo. Explain that they are now going to make a ceramic form based on their studies.

Demonstrate how to roll out clay so that it is half an inch thick. Then they can carefully draw around their hand with a modelling tool and finally a knife. By doing this, they will have the advantage of starting with the clay the correct length to create a hand (Figure 18D).

18D

Now they should smooth away the hard edges to make the fingers rounded and build up the inside of the model until it compares with the thickness of their own hand. Work on the inside first (Figure 18E) and then turn the model over.

18E

It is now a good idea to rest the model on a cushion of newspaper while they work on the back. The important thing is to make sure the fingers only bend at the joints. Building up an angled joint will greatly help to create realism (Figure 18F).

18F

47

It is important that the child arranges the model in its desired position before the end of this session. Even if it is far from being finished, as long as the work is supported with crushed newspaper and carefully wrapped in a polythene bag, it will keep in good condition for at least a month. As the model nears completion, encourage the children to work to a high standard... adding fine details, smoothing rough edges and so on.

When it is 'as good as it can be', check that areas such as the wrist are not too thick before firing. If, as is usually the case, the clay on the wrist is thicker than one inch across, simply hollow it out in the middle.

Make sure the models are thoroughly dried before firing.

Homework 2

Get the children to make a drawing of their model the way they hope it will look when its finished.

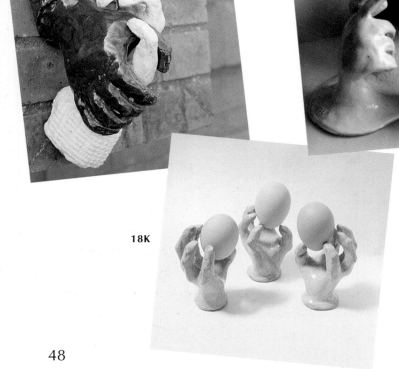

18H

18I

18K

S E S S I O N 4

Glazing

Starting Point

Show the children how to glaze their work (See Part 3 Techniques.) They should write notes on their drawing to indicate the glazes they have used.

Figures 18G to 18K are examples of children's work.

18G

18J

Development

One child decided hands could be used as egg cups as illustrated in Figure 18K.

Evaluation

Were the children successful in completing a model? How sensitive was the modelling? Did the model manage to convey an idea?

48

19 PORTRAIT HEADS

SESSION 1

Drawing from observation

Starting Point

Introduce the subject by looking at the work of various sculptors. Why has Epstein left the surface of some sculptures rough and others smooth? How have various people modelled the eye to create an idea of depth in the iris? How has Rodin managed to convey the idea of movement or emotion in his figures?

Divide the class into pairs so that they can study each other.

Give out paper and tell the children to take turns to draw. It is best to time them for fifteen-minute sessions. The person who is being drawn must sit absolutely still and they swop after fifteen minutes. It helps to talk them through the drawing. This enables them to concentrate on details and it helps them all to work at the same rate.

At the end of an hour they should all have finished (Figure 19A).

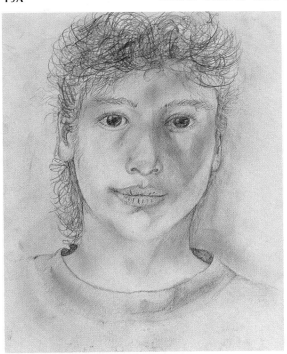

19A

Homework 1

Ask the children to go to the library and make a sketch of the various ways in which sculptors have modelled or carved facial details. They should take care to note down the names of the sculptors they have studied.

SESSION 2

Making the armature

Starting Point

Each child needs to have his own armature (Figure 19B). Once one class of children has made a set of armatures they will last for several years with only occasional repair, so this session needs only to be done once.

19B

Give each child a square of wood approximately 6–9 inches wide to form the base, and another piece of wood approximately 12 inches long and 1–2 inches thick to form the stand.

Show them how to place the stand in the middle of the base and hammer two or three long nails to hold them together. It is important that this join is very secure because the clay will be very heavy once they begin to build on top.

Give every child two pieces of heavy-duty wire approximately one foot long. Show them how to join the wire onto the stand using U-shaped nails. The two pieces of wire must cross over at the top to form a hollow ball. Thinner wire can be worked between them to hold the whole shape firmly. Crushed newspaper is now pushed inside the wire to fill it completely and the whole wire structure is covered with several thicknesses of newspaper to enable the clay to come away easily when the model is finished.

SESSION 3

Modelling the head

Starting Point

Gather the class around your table and show them how to add newspaper to the armature, then how to roll out the clay to cover the frame. (See Figures 19C and 19D.)

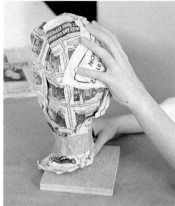

19C

19D

19E

They should use a tape measure to make sure that they make the head the correct circumference, and they should get the shape of the head right before they begin to work on the features. (See Figure 19E.)

19F

The hair can be added by rolling strips of clay and then texturing it with a fork (Figures 19F and 19G).

Eye lids need to be built up over the eye ball (Figure 19G).

Although initially it is a good idea for them to refer to their partner for anatomical details, it will probably be more fun to make their head a 'character', based on the way it seems to be coming rather than trying to produce an accurate likeness of their friend.

19G

At the end of each session the work should be covered with a polythene bag to prevent it from drying out.

Homework 2

Ask the children to make a drawing of the character they are modelling in clay (Figure 19H).

19H

50

SESSION 4

Removing the armature

Starting Point

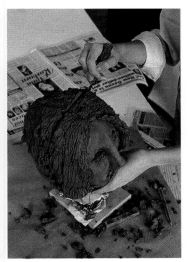

Once the main features have been established and the clay has had time become 'leather-hard', it is time to cut it from the frame. It is best to make the cut across the hair to prevent damage to the face (Figure 19I).

Gently ease the two halves of the model off the frame and rest them on a cushion of crumpled newspaper (Figure 19J). Now that it is in half, check that there are no areas thicker than an inch. If there are, these must be hollowed out. Score the areas of the join and paint them with slip (liquid clay) to act as a glue (Figure 19K).

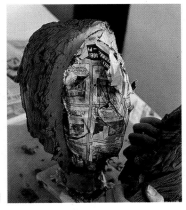

19J

19K

Now push both halves together again and work the join until it disappears. (It is best to use somebody's model to demonstrate this and then run around helping those in trouble.) The model will probably need to have extra clay added to the neck to enable it to stand and some of the details will need to be re-worked. It is probably a good idea to wait until it has been cut off before working in too much detail. Ears and hair are often best left until now.

The model will need at least a week drying before any attempt is made to fire it.

SESSION 5

Glazing

Starting Point

19L

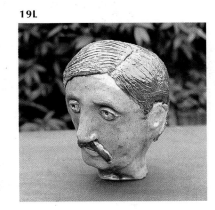

Show the children how to paint the glazes on. They should make notes of the glazes they have used so they can review how successful they are after firing.

Figures 19L and 19M are examples of children's work.

19M

Evaluation

Were the children successful in completing their model? Were they able to give it a character? Did they manage to apply the glaze appropriately? Are there aspects of the work that show how the child has been influenced by looking at the work of other sculptors?

SESSION 1

Researching   20A

Starting Point

Show the children examples of sculpture where the sculptor has taken the human form and produced a work that is powerfully expressive. Rodin is excellent for this purpose.

Explain that they are going to make a model of a human being that can tell a story. They can decide on the story, but it should be 'about' something.

Demonstrate a method of working with clay that the children can relate to easily. If they begin by joining thin coils together to form limbs rather like a pipe-cleaner man, they will have a good base to build upon. They can either add additional clay to build up muscles or roll thin sheets of clay to make clothes (Figure 20B).

20B

Encourage them to experiment with this method of working during the first session.

Homework 1

The children should decide what their model is going to be about.

SESSIONS 2 & 3

Modelling

Starting Point

Help the children to develop their individual work.

Figures 20A, and 20C to 20E are examples of children's work.

Dean's very simple figure has been given texture by rolling the clay onto crochet (Figure 20A).

20C

Joanne produced a model that would demonstrate the passage of time. An old man and a boy are sat on a seat. They are the same person sitting on the same seat at two different times in his life. Behind him is the street and we can see how it has changed over the past sixty years (Figure 20C).

Sharon made a huge model of two tramps sitting in a drunken stupor (Figure 20D).

Emma made three models, each expressing varying degrees of freedom. One is completely encased in leaves, another is beginning to break free and the third is rejoicing in his nakedness (Figure 20E).

Evaluation

Have the children managed to produce a model? Does it have character? Is it able to express an idea?

20E

21 STILL LIFE

21A

SESSION 1

Drawing from observation

Starting Point

Set up a large still-life group in the centre of the room and arrange the seating so that all the children have a good view. Try to find a large variety of textures and shapes: plants, coloured fabric, chrome, glass, musical instruments, etc. (Figure 21A).

Give the children cardboard windows to use as viewers. They use these to isolate the area they are going to draw.

The children draw their area as accurately as possible.

Homework 1

Get the children to make another cardboard window and draw a small section of one room in their home.

SESSIONS 2 & 3

Adding colour

The children continue with their drawings and begin to add colour. They can choose any

21B medium:, paint, dry pastel, oil pastel or coloured pencil (Figure 21B).

Homework 2

The children should find magazine pictures, coloured papers, cloth, etc. which will help them with their collage next week.

SESSION 4

Collage

Starting Point

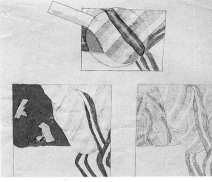

21C

Show examples of absract art (e.g. Mondrian), then show the children how to select an area of their picture to develop into a new medium. This area must be translated into a collage. If there is time, children could experiment with several different types of collage: tissue paper; magazine photographs; scraps of cloth, etc. The collage should emphasise one aspect of their original picture, (colour, texture, shape, etc.). It will involve them in abstracting one element. (Examples are shown in Figures 21C and 21D.) This can now be developed into a design for a clay tile or panel in a slab pot.

21D

Homework 3

The children should find materials that can provide interesting surfaces for their clay work (e.g. the string bags that oranges are sold in, hessian, tree bark, textured wallpaper, knitted and woven fabrics, etc.).

SESSION 5

Texture tile

Starting Point

Collect all the textured surfaces together and show the children how to experiment to produce a range of different textures by embedding material into the clay.

21E

Demonstrate how to roll out a slab of clay and cut it to make a 'picture frame' with mitred edges. This mitred edge will prevent the picture from falling out if the narrow opening is in the front (Figure 21E).

The pupils can now recreate the shapes of their collage in terms of textured surfaces, which are carefully laid into the frame and joined at the back. Soft clay is used to fill in the back. This can be used as one side of a slab pot.

Show the children examples of slab pots by contemporary potters and photographs of slab-moulded lamp bases, etc.

Homework 4

Ask the children to design their own slab pot.

SESSION 6

Designing a slab pot

Starting Point

Show the children how to make a paper template to plan their pot. A simple design would be to roll out another side the same size as their textured tile and two more the same height and half the width. (If the children roll the clay between wooden guides, they can be sure they will be of equal thickness.)

All the slabs, (minimum four sides and a base), should be rolled out this session and then laid between absorbent paper and placed in a polythene bag ready to assemble next week. They need to be 'leather-hard'.

SESSION 7

Constructing

Starting Point

Show the children how to join the sides together. Both edges to be joined should be scored with a knife and glued with liquid clay. A thin coil of clay worked into

21F

the join will help to hold it together (Figure 21F).

It will take the whole of this session to assemble the pots.

The work must be allowed to dry slowly before it is fired in the kiln. If it dries too quickly the join is likely to come apart.

SESSION 8

Glazing

Starting Point

Glazes should be carefully painted on to make the most of the textured panel. The children should make careful notes of the glazes they have used to compare the finished result with their expectations.

Figures 21G and 21H are examples of children's work. The pot in Figure 21G Gillian based on the studies of collages in Session 4. Joanne's pot is based on her own studies (Figure 21H).

This method of working may be used to produce a lino print or a weaving (Figure 21I).

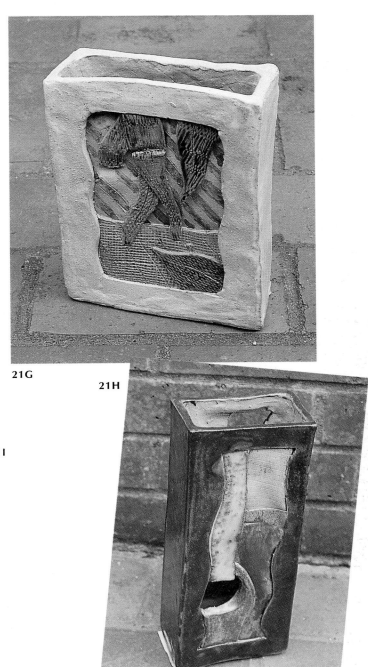

21G

21H

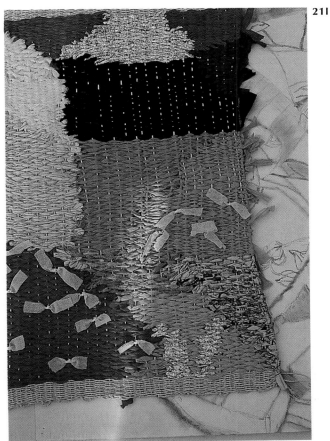

21I

Evaluation

Were the children able to record accurately during their initial observation? Were they able to abstract elements from that drawing to work as a collage? Were they able to translate their collage into a textured window in clay? Did they manage to construct a slab pot and glaze it appropriately?

SESSION 1

Reseaching

Starting Point

Begin the lesson by looking at paintings where the artist has adopted an unusual viewpoint. Lucian Freud has painted a number of portraits where we find ourselves looking up at the subject as though we are sitting on the ground, and others as though we were looking down from the ceiling. This is very disturbing, since the majority of portraits offer eye-to-eye contact. Stanley Spencer also offers an unusual viewpoint in his pictures and so too does the Renaissance painter Mantegna.

Talk about different viewpoints. What do we look like from the point of view of a bird? What sort of view would we have of the classroom if we were sitting on the ceiling?

Show examples of aerial photographs. Have the children ever been in an aeroplane? What did the world look like from there? Give out photographs of birds in flight. This is their starting point. They should begin by drawing the bird as carefully as possible in one corner of an A2 sheet and then carefully planning the view it might have from there. Is it flying over the town or countryside?

Homework 1

The children continue planning for their picture. They bring in pictures from home: newspaper and magazine cuttings, as well as any photographs taken from aeroplanes or ski lifts (Figure 22A).

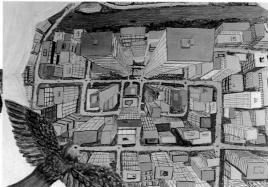

22A

SESSIONS 2 & 3

Composition

Starting Point

22B

Review Homework 1 together. Ask the children to plan out their pictures, remembering that the objects nearest to them need to be drawn larger than those which are further away. This will be contrary to the normal view they have of buildings. The tops of buildings will be bigger than the base. Instead of looking up at them, they must imagine what it would be like to look down.

Let the children work on their pictures until they are happy with the result.

22C

Anthony produced a bird's eye view of pollution (Figure 22B).

Joanne worked on a bird's eye view of the countryside (Figure 22C).

Then she worked on a complex view of the town (Figure 22D).

22D

SESSION 4

Development

Starting Point

Ask the children to choose one section of their picture to look at in detail. They must simplify it into a simple shape that can be repeated as a pattern.

Joanne chose to work on a group of six buildings next to a roundabout. By using the idea of the roadway and the roundabout she is able to use the same six shapes to produce a repeat pattern. The road is the linking device and she can line it up easily by forming the central circle of the roundabout when the quarters match up (Figure 22E).

A country view could also work by using the lines of hedges and field patterns in a similar way.

Once the design has been worked out it can be produced as a silk-screen print (Figures 22F and 22G).

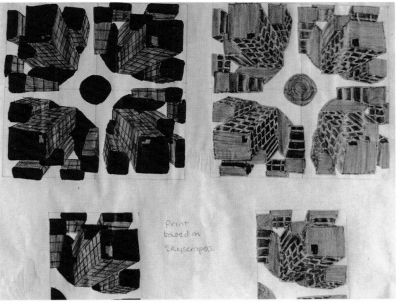

22E

22F

22G

Joanne printed hers in black and white on a blue sheet. Each colour requires a separate stencil and the linking stencil (the black roundabout) must be printed first. (See Part 3 Techniques for details of silk-screen printing.

Evaluation

Were the children able to understand the idea of a changed viewpoint? Were they able to develop individual work based on the idea?

SESSION 1

Research

Starting Point

Describe a world of peasants living and working in a rural community where the church would be the only stone building for miles around. Describe it as a landmark, its tower dwarfing all surrounding structures; a place of overwhelming space and light compared to simple peasant dwellings, where everyone met once a week and could wonder at the treasures of Heaven depicted in the stained glass windows and shudder at the goblins of Hell spouting water from the roof.

Describe a truly utilitarian architecture based on 'state of the art' civil engineering and contrast the mastery of the pointed arch and the science of vaulting a church by means of crosswise arches.

Show the children examples of these features either from slides or books and then describe the features to look for on their visit to their local church.

SESSION 2

Drawing from observation

Preparation

Well before this visit is planned, permission must be obtained from the vicar and from the children's parents. Refer to Part 2 Planning a Visit.

Starting Point

Take the children on a tour of the building, pointing out the interesting aspects as you pass them. Let them choose an area they would like to study.

23A

Give out drawing boards so that children can work comfortably and encourage them to work from careful observation (Figure 23A).

Pastels are a very useful medium to record colour directly since they are very easy to use. However, a small box of watercolour paints need not be too difficult so long as they have a small container for water.

23C

Kelli produced the pastel study of a window, shown in Figure 23B, during her visit, while Jacob produced his window in watercolour (Figure 23C).

23B

Before leaving the site, all the children should have an opportunity to photograph the area they have been working from. One 36-exposure film can be shared by the class and will be an invaluable resource back at school.

Homework 1

The children should plan how they might develop a piece of artwork based on their visit.

If possible, the children could come back after school in groups of six to print their photograph in the school's darkroom.

SESSION 3

Development

Starting Point

Review the work achieved on-site together with the photographs. How can the work be developed from here?

David, Kelli and Rachel went on to produce paintings based on their studies. They began working on them at the church and completed them back at school (Figures 23D, 23E and 23F).

Katie produced a ceramic tile based on a stained-glass window (Figure 23G) and then went on to use the window design again in two night lights (Figure 23H).

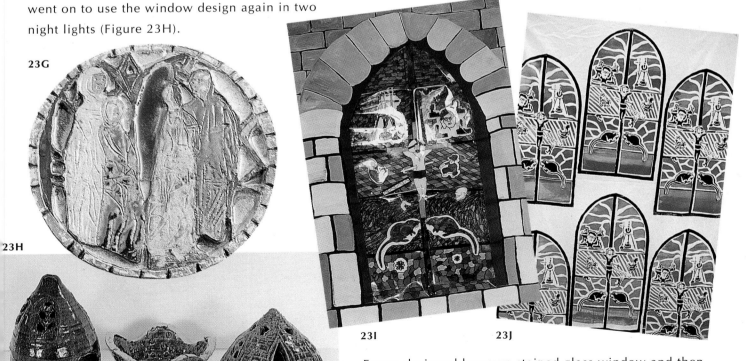

23D

23E

23F

23G

23H

23I

23J

Emma designed her own stained glass window and then went on to produce a silk-screen print based on it (Figures 23I and 23J).

Carl made a large ceramic model of the church (Figure 23K) and then went on to work on a sgraffito tile based on a design from the font (Figure 23L).

Julie made sgraffito tiles based on different views of her local church (Figure 23M).

23K

23L

23M
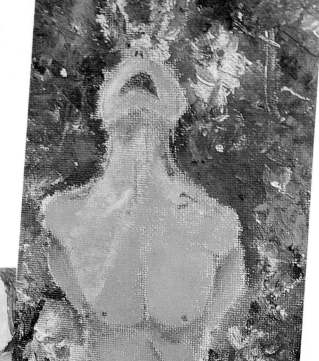
23N

David became very involved in Christian symbolism and went on to study painters such as Sutherland and Bacon who have worked on versions of the crucifixion. David then produced his own paintings on the same theme (Figures 23N and 23O).

23O

Evaluation

Were the children able to work well from direct observation?

Were they able to develop their initial studies into a successful piece of work?

24 FASTENINGS

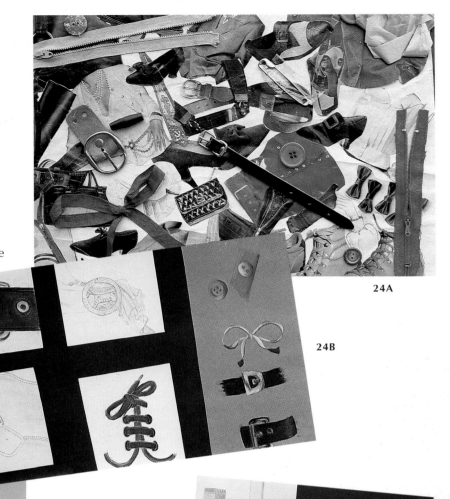

24A

SESSION 1

Investigating

Starting Point

Provide a whole range of fastenings: zips; buttons; velcro; press studs; laces, etc.(Figure 24A). Ask the children to make careful drawings of them from observation. They can work with a range of media. Oil pastel could be used to create the sheen on velvet, etc.(Figure 24B).

24B

Homework 1

Ask the children to bring in a whole range of fastenings from home and, using a sketch pad, plan a way that the fastenings can be used to create an unusual design. What could be fastened together using buttons, etc? They have all heard of unzipping a banana. What would a banana look like with a zip?

24C

24D

SESSION 2

Designing

Starting Point

Show the work of surrealist artists. Magritte makes many visual puns similar to the one they are about to make with their fastenings.

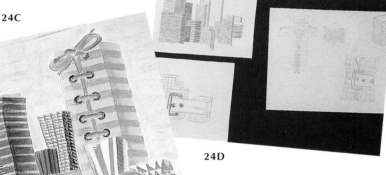

24E

Help the children to find a suitable outcome.

A PICTURE

Figure 24C shows how Claire has imagined a city held together with fastenings. She began by drawing a high-rise skyline and then working out ways of combining the images (Figures 24D and 24E). Her final pastel picture is very amusing.

Gill has used the same idea and developed it onto a sgraffito tile (Figure 24F).

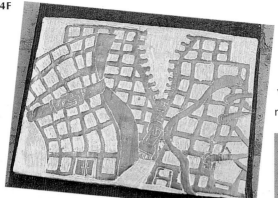

24F

Gillian decided to see what a banana would look like if it were unzipped to reveal a carrot (Figure 24K).

24K

A PRINT

Neil set up an arrangement of articles that contained fastenings so that they formed an interesting group (Figure 24G). He then traced his picture to produce a simple design for a print (Figure 24H).

24G

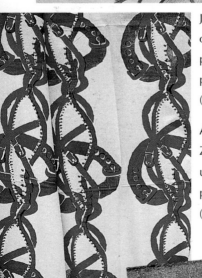

24H

She went on to make an animated film based on this idea. This involved her in drawing the whole process in careful stages. It took thirty drawings to enable the banana to unpeel itself. These had to be carefully lined up, so that when the filming was done it would look as though the original drawing was changing. The film was shot on Super 8 allowing two frames to be taken for each image. This produced the appearance of continuous movement (Figure 24L).

24L

Jane used her arrangement of zips and buckles to produce a bold silk-screen print for a length of fabric (Figure 24I).

A CERAMIC OUTCOME

Zoe used the idea of unzipping an eye to produce a ceramic tile (Figure 24J).

24I

24J

Evaluation

Were the children able to produce good drawings from observation? Were they able to develop these into a work of their own? How were they influenced by studying the surrealists?

SESSIONS 1 & 2

Drawing from observation

Starting Point

Introduce the subject by showing examples of work by Surrealist artists: Dali, Magritte, Ernst and Miro.

Explain to the class that they are going to work on two images which will converge to form something completely new. They are going to work on the idea of combining machine parts with the human form: a sort of robotic image.

Ideally a visit to the local scrapyard or municipal dump can be very useful. This would enable children to select their own machine parts and to take photographs of their choice (Figure 25A).

25A

This first session requires a large variety of machine parts and PCBs for the children to work

from. Encourage them to produce accurate drawings by looking carefully before making any marks on their paper (Figure 25B).

By the end of two sessions they should have a number of careful studies they can work from.

25B

Homework 1

Get the children to make a careful drawing of figures, either themselves by looking in a mirror, or drawings of family and friends. They should plan how to combine these studies with the machine parts; perhaps by having an area of skin missing (Figure 25C).

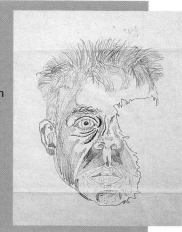

25C

SESSIONS 3 & 4

Combining images

Starting Point

Review the drawings from last week and the Homework 1 and suggest ways to combine the two images together.

Give out A2 paper and show the children how

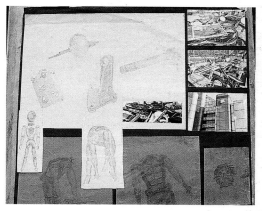

25D

to use the mechanical shapes they have drawn to replace anatomical detail. If they use tracing paper, it is easy to superimpose one image onto another (Figure 25D).

In Figure 25E, a motorbike's cooling system has been combined with the human heart.

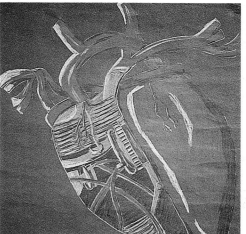

25E

Marie has used her studies of machine parts to form a robot and has used the photographs she took to make the figure come to life on the municipal dump. She went on to produce a screen print based on this image (Figures 25F, 25G and 25H).

25G

25F

25H

25I

Development

This idea of combining images together can be used in many contexts. Steven has produced Zebraphants by combining certain characteristics of both animals together (Figure 25I).

Glen has combined an eye with legs to create a monster, as shown in Figure 25J.

Sharon has made a model to describe how someone can change to look like their pet (Figures 25K and 25L).

25J

25K

25L

Evaluation

Were the children able to combine two images to form a new creature? How were they influenced by studies of other artists? Were they able to develop their initial ideas into their own work?

26A

SESSION 1

Drawing from observation

Starting Point

Introduce the subject by looking at a range of fabric designs, not only designs by William Morris, but also contemporary fabrics with a view to discovering the source of the original idea.

26B

Provide the children with a wide range of natural forms: flowers; seed pods; wood bark; shells; skulls and animal bones.

Ask them to make careful studies of these in a range of media. See Figures 26A, 26B, 26C and 26D, pencil, dry pastel, oil pastel and acrylic paint.

Homework 1

Suggest that the children look at fabric designs at home and decide from what they were derived.

26D

26C

S E S S I O N 2

Designing

Starting Point

Ask the children to look carefully at the last session's drawings and begin to simplify them, concentrating on pattern and line. See how Marie has begun to simplify the daffodils to work out a design (Figure 26E). Working in monotone can help children to isolate simple shapes and lines.

26E

26F

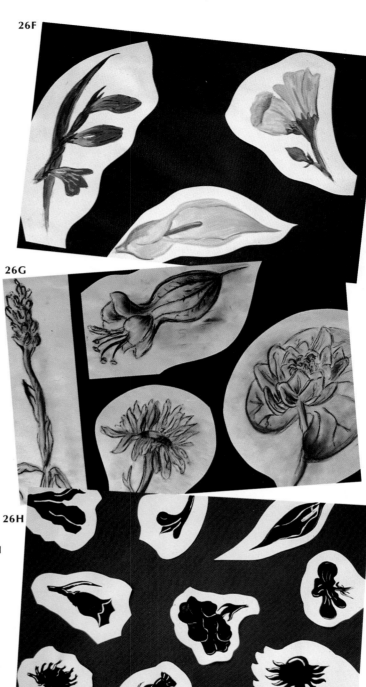

26G

26H

26I

Caroline began by painting flowers in watercolour, then she worked in charcoal and finally black paint, working on the silhouettes. This gave her clear shapes which she could translate into a simple stencil (Figures 26F, G, H and I). Refer to the section on silk-screen printing in Part 3 Techniques.

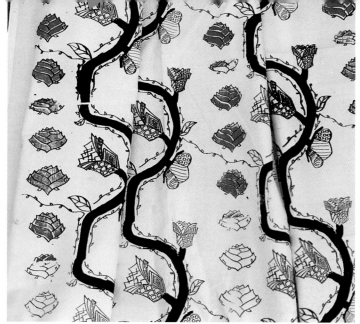

26K

Claire worked out an abstract design based on rose buds shown in Figures 26J and 26K.

26J

Ingrid produced a bold three-coloured print based on her arrangement of fruit (Figures 26L and 26M).

26L

26M

Homework 2

Ask the children to work out a way to produce a design that will repeat.

SESSION 3

Designing

Starting Point

Demonstrate a way of producing a design that will link together. The simplest way to do this is by using a device such as a stem. (See Part 3 Techniques).

Once the child has produced a design, he or she must check that it will fit together correctly. Then a decision should be made about the colours to use. It is probably best to use a maximum of three colours.

Once the design is finalised, it is time to begin to cut the paper stencils: one stencil for each colour. It is important that the linking stencil (e.g. the stem and any other areas using the same colour) is printed first.

SESSIONS 4 & 5

Printing

Refer to Part 3 Techniques.

Evaluation

Were the children able to abstract designs from natural forms? Were they able to develop their initial studies into a design suitable for printing?

SESSION 1

Drawing from observation

Starting Point

The children work in Session 1 as for a printed outcome, that is, using a wide range of media to explore the shapes and textures of a range of natural forms: fruit; seeds; shells; leaves, etc. Show them examples of ceramic forms from contemporary and primitive potters who have worked on this theme.

Homework 1

Ask the children to find examples of natural forms which would make a good design for a vessel, for example, rosehips, gourds, shells, acorns, poppy heads, etc.

SESSION 2

Researching

Starting Point

Review the children's work from the last session and the drawings and objects they have brought in as homework. How could they go about building forms such as these using clay?

Demonstrate three very simple techniques:

27A

1 Rolling clay out into a leaf shape that is then shaped into a curved bowl by arranging newspaper around it to hold it in place as it dries (Figure 27A).

2 Pushing your thumb into a ball of clay and hollowing it out to form a simple thumb pot (Figure 27B).

27B

3 Using the two mould dishes and sandwiching them together with slip to form a hollow vessel (Figure 27C).

27C

Ask the children to decide on their preferred form and work on one of these techniques to produce a model of their own in clay.

Karen used mould dishes to produce her pots based on shell designs (Figures 27D and 27E).

SECTIONS OF ENLARGED SHELLS

27D

27E

Sally has used leaf shapes cut out of clay and then fitted together to form pots (Figure 27F).

Chloe has worked on the same idea but one leaf makes a dish (Figure 27G).

27F

27G

27H

Julie's studies of seed pods and fruit have been developed into ceramic forms using the thumb pot technique (Figure 27H).

27I

The apple has New York's skyscrapers inside, a symbol of the 'big apple' itself (Figure 27I).

Evaluation

Were the children able to develop the characteristic shapes of natural form into ceramics? Were they able to develop work based on their initial drawings? Did they manage to keep the essential qualities of the forms they were studying when they applied glazes?

SESSION 1

Drawing from observation

Starting Point

Begin by showing examples of still-life painting. Although it is good to show a variety of styles, it is useful to include some 16th-Century Dutch and Flemish masters. Allow the children to experiment with a range of media to capture the qualities of fruit, flowers, bone, shell, wood, etc (Figures 28A and 28B).

The first session should be given over to research and experimentation with colour in the form of paint thickened with PVA, watercolour, oil pastel and dry pastel (Figure 28C).

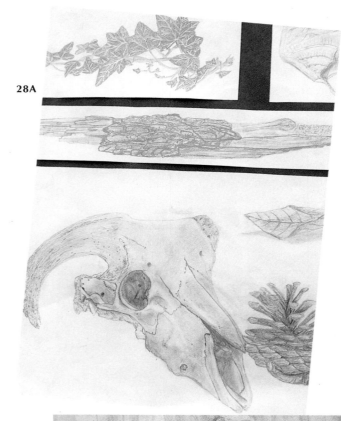

28A

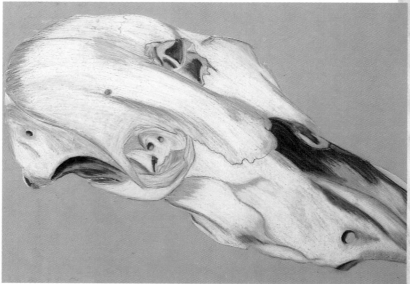

28B

28C

Homework 1

The children should plan the picture they would like to work on next session and decide which of the media they intend using.

S E S S I O N S 2 , 3 & 4

28D

Painting

S t a r t i n g   P o i n t

Encourage the children to set up groups of objects they will be happy to work on for the next three weeks and to use 'study sheets' to experiment with colour effects. Marie experimented with painting apples before working on her main picture (Figures 28D and 28E).

28E

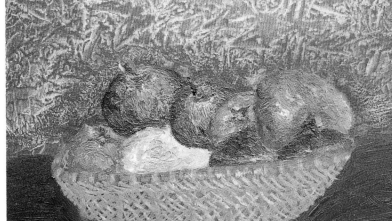

The examples here show a range of media. Helen developed her study of skulls into an imaginative composition (Figure 28F). While Marie was content to capture a vase of flowers (Figure 28G).

28F

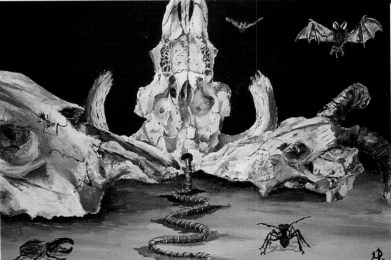

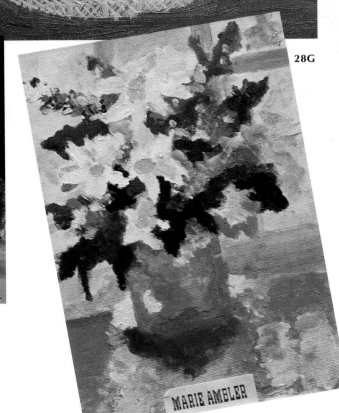

28G

E v a l a u t i o n

Were the children able to capture the form, textures and colours of natural form in their use of paint? How were they influenced by the artists they studied?

MARIE AMBLER

SESSIONS 1 & 2

Slide show

Starting Point

Arrange a slide show of a few of the paintings that will be available at the gallery and introduce the children to a creative way of looking at pictures. Encourage them to tell you what the pictures are about by using the clues in the picture rather than simply telling them. 'What's happening in this picture?' 'Are the people happy or is something wrong?' 'How do you know that?' When you have looked at the meaning behind the picture, get the children to look at the technique. 'How has the artist created a feeling of space, movement or light?'

Give out photocopies of famous paintings: the Impressionists and Van Gogh are ideal and the fact they have been reduced to monochrome will make this work easier. Suggest that they can either work on black paper and use white paint or vice versa. They must copy the photocopy by painting directly on the paper, imitating the artist's use of brush strokes.

Figures 29A, 29B and 29C are examples of children's work.

SESSION 3

Visit to the gallery

Preparation

It is very important that the children are given guidance both before and during their visit. If possible arrange for them to have a guided tour by one of the gallery staff. These people are extremely skilled in introducing paintings to children and they know how to involve them in active looking. If a guided tour is not available, then you should devise a worksheet that will involve them in looking carefully at the pictures. Without a device of this sort, it is perfectly possible for the children to wonder around and 'see' nothing! Refer to Part 2 Planning a Visit.

Ask the children to buy at least one postcard of an artist they particularly like, because they will need it to work from during their next lesson.

29A 29B 29C

Homework 1

Ask the children to go to the library to find the painting section and to select a painting they particularly like and write a description of it including details such as the artist's name, the title, the date of painting and so on.

Homework 2

Suggest that the children use the library again to find out about other paintings by their chosen artist. Ask them to think about a way of developing a piece of work based on his or her work.

SESSION 4

Transcription

Starting Point

Ask the class to copy, at least, a small section of the postcard they have chosen. They should work to a larger scale than the postcard and they might find it helpful to divide the image into a grid in order to enlarge it. They should try to copy the colours and the way the artist has used paint as carefully as possible.

Before the end of this session suggest ways in which this work may be developed into different outcomes, for example, a painting using the paint in the same way as the artist or a similar subject to the artist; a silk-screen print based on images the artist has used or a ceramic mural based on elements of the artist's work.

Homework 3

Ask the children to plan the development of next session's work.

29F

29G

29H

SESSION 5

Development

29D

A PAINTED OUTCOME

This is on the surface the most simple development, but it can lead to some very exciting work. A vase of flowers, painted with PVA mixed into the paint to give it a thick texture to imitate Van Gogh's Sunflowers, can be very impressive. The child working from real flowers is trying to work in a bold, free way (Figure 29D). Figure 29E is a still-life arrangement similar to one by the Dutch masters, including the child's choice of objects.

29E

A PRINTED OUTCOME

Here the child selects a number of images from an artist's work and uses them in a design of her or his own.

Sharon was very impressed with the work of William Blake. She began by copying the details she liked and then found an image of cherubs which she was able to incorporate in a design for a silk-screen print (Figures 29F, G, H and I). See Part 3 Techniques.

29I

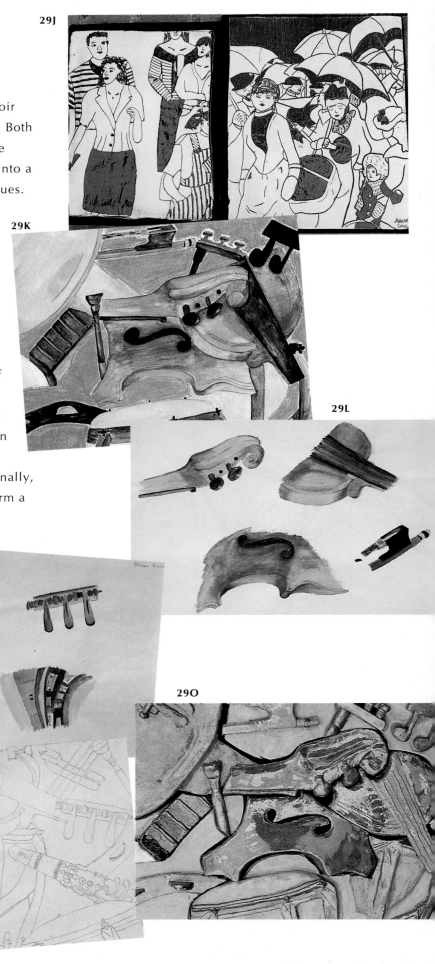

29J

A CERAMIC OUTCOME

Here Maxine has selected a painting by Renoir and updated it to a summer day in the 1990s. Both her transcription of Renoir's painting and the contemporary version have been translated into a sgraffito tile (Figure 29J). See Part 3 Techniques.

A CUBIST OUTCOME

29K

Children often latch on to the idea that they can use the technique employed by the cubists to include all the things they like about a subject by juxtaposing various aspects of it in one picture (Figure 29K).

Here Gillian has taken the theme of musical instruments. She began by making studies of various instruments we had at school, selecting the parts that she thought were the most interesting (Figures 29L and 29M). Then she planned various ways they could be arranged together to make a good design. Finally, she modelled them in clay so they would form a ceramic relief (Figures 29N and 29O).

29L

29M

Evaluation

Were the children able to use imaginatively some of the methods and approaches used by the artists they studied at the gallery? Were they able to develop their own work based on the discoveries they made?

29N

29O

PART 2 PLANNING A VISIT

If you are planning to take a group of children out for a whole day, you will probably need to make all the initial bookings at least six weeks before you go.

The first person to ask is your headteacher to support and approve the idea and to check with the school diary to find a suitable day to go.

Having obtained consent, phone the gallery or museum to see if they will be able to accommodate you on that day and provisionally book gallery staff for a guided tour. The National Gallery and the Tate Gallery offer excellent tours that cost you nothing. Other places may charge a small fee, but they are well worth it.

The next thing to do is to organise transport. It is well worth phoning around to see what a number of coach companies will charge for the journey. There is often a considerable difference in quotes. This also needs to be provisionally booked at this stage.

If children stay for canteen lunches, send a note to the kitchen to inform them of your plans.

Pencil in the information into the school diary and inform colleagues who might be affected on that day.

Writing a letter to the parents needs to be considered carefully, because unless the school is able to fund the trip without parental assistance, it will be necessary to ask for voluntary contributions. Work out the number of voluntary contributions that will be necessary to cover the cost of the trip and explain in your letter that unless sufficient contributions are received the trip will be cancelled.

The letter also needs to make clear to parents the time of arrival and departure from the museum, the method of transport and how you have organised the children's day. If a packed lunch is required, this needs to be made clear, as too should the type of clothing to be worn on the day. If school uniform is required, it will help you identify your group easily, but I find children behave in a more adult manner when they are visiting museums and galleries in their own clothes. I do, however, specify they should wear 'smart casual clothing'.

The bottom of the letter should contain a reply slip so that you have parental consent in writing.

Once initial plans have been finalised, inform the rest of the staff so they are fully aware of your plans and confirm bookings with the gallery and bus company. Make arrangements to take additional staff (the current regulations require one adult to fifteen children).

If the visit is to be truly worthwhile the children ought to do some preparatory work. I usually make a point of showing a number of the paintings from the gallery before we go so that the children will be familiar with them on the day. It is best to try to get the children to tell you about the paintings by using visual clues. This involves them in thinking rather than simply listening and will give them the skills to look at paintings on their own.

If a guided tour is unavailable, or if you want the children to look for specific things on their visit, you need to provide a worksheet. Visit the museum or gallery shortly before you bring the children to check the exhibits and the layout of the building. Design the sheet to take them on a trail.

The day before the visit, gather together all the children you are taking and make sure they understand what is required of them in terms of practical details and behaviour. Check the kitchen are aware or your arrangements and display the names of the children involved on the staff noticeboard. Make arrangements to take the school's First Aid kit (and sick bucket). Make sure any children you are leaving behind are adequately catered for with work and that any teachers covering your lessons are quite happy.

Before leaving school on the day of the trip, give the school office an accurate list of all the people travelling on the coach together with the number of the coach you are using.

Now that you have planned it all properly you have nothing to do but enjoy yourself!

*P*ART **3**

*T*ECHNIQUES

PRINTING

There are many methods of printing, from simple mono prints to elaborate silk-screen printing. All of them require pre-planning to produce a suitable design.

Mono printing

The simplest form of printing is simply to roll block printing ink out onto a smooth surface and to draw into it. A pencil will give fine lines, fingers will give thicker more expressive ones. The children draw out their picture in the ink

TA

and then lay a sheet of paper on top to make a print. Animal shapes can be very exciting produced in this way (See Figure TA).

Cardboard relief printing

Here the children are each given a square of cardboard and encouraged to build up a textural surface by glueing on string, fabric, plastic bubbles, etc. This works best if the children have drawn their design first and then they translate it into a textural relief. PVA is excellent for glueing a whole variety of materials together. It takes a few days to dry properly so the printing block needs to be completed in one session and the printing needs to be done during the following one. Block printing ink is rolled onto the surface of the block and then pressed onto the paper (Figure TB).

TB

Lino Printing

It is possible to plan to build up several layers of colour using this technique.

Children plan their design on paper and then draw it out onto the lino tile. They must take very great care using the lino tools. Show them how to use the wooden blocks to hold the tile still and how they must always use the tool away from themselves. It is possible for them

TC

to cut themselves badly if they do not listen to this advice (Figure TC).

When sufficient areas of the tile have been removed they are ready to print the first colour.

TD

Squeeze block printing ink out on to a sheet of plastic or hardboard and roll the colour onto the tile (Figures TD and TE). Place the tile down onto the paper and with a clean roller, roll the back to make sure the ink has made good contact (Figure TF).

TE

TF

Carefully lift the tile to avoid smudging (Figure TG).

They can plan an interesting way of repeating the design by experimenting with its position.

When they have printed the first colour, the tile can be washed and more of it can be cut away to allow another colour to be printed on top. Make sure the first colour is dry before printing the second.

Silk-screen printing

This requires the most planning, but it can yield very professional results.

The screen

The silk-screen is simply a wooden frame with fine nylon mesh stretched over it. The frame has to be very strong and commercially produced ones are available, but the mesh can be stretched on without too much difficulty. I buy the appropriate mesh from ' Sericol' or 'GHS', and cut it to size and stretch it when wet, using staples to hold it in place. The mesh needs to be a little bigger than the frame in all directions and

any raw edges should be turned under as they are tacked onto the sides. I usually work with my colleague, one of us keeping the mesh taut while the other works with the staple gun. We fix on one of the long sides first, then work on the opposite side of the frame to pull it under tension. Once stretched, the mesh will serve for many prints as long as the ink is washed out before it gets a chance to dry. I suggest using water soluble inks. Before printing it is necessary to stick a length of gum strip inside the screen at the place where the frame and the mesh meet to prevent any ink leakage from that join.

Stencils

The principle of silk-screen printing is the same as stencilling. Ink is pulled across the mesh using a squeegee, but where the screen is blocked the ink cannot pass through. A separate stencil is needed for each colour (Figure TI).

The simplest stencils are cut out of paper. Good quality paper needs to be used for this to prevent ink seeping through. The child works out his or her design so a separate stencil may be cut for each colour. If a free-standing shape like 'O' is cut, the centre needs a tie to hold it in place. In practice the ink will hold it in place once the first ink has been pulled through (but the child needs to keep the middle and set it up exactly where the print is wanted). Paper stencils are fine for short run prints.

Figure TH shows Emma using a craft knife to cut out the second stencil for her print. She is cutting it out of a sheet of paper that has the first print on it so she knows it will match up.

If greater precision is required, there are a number of manufacturers who provide excellent stencil materials.

It is possible to buy a special film for hand-cut stencils. These stencils have two layers. The upper layer has the design cut from it, but is supported throughout by a backing sheet. When the stencil is ironed onto the screen, the upper layer will adhere to its surface and the backing sheet will come away.

Photographic stencils allow for very fine details to be printed. Designs are painted with opaque black paint onto tracing paper and then placed in contact with an indirect photostencil film and exposed to ultraviolet light in a controlled environment. Where the light is able to pass through the tracing paper the stencil will harden, but the areas that were painted black will not allow the light to penetrate and so will wash out after development. The stencil will then adhere to the screen and will print perfectly once it has had time to dry.

Printing

Cover a table with newspaper and have everything required at hand.

- Gum strip (to fill in any holes that appear in the stencil)
- Paper towels or sugar paper (to protect printed sections from the screen)
- Screen-printing ink
- Squeegee
- Spoon (to take ink from container)
- Paper or cloth to print on to.

If using a paper stencil, set it up on a plain sheet of paper in exactly the position required for the

TJ

finished print. Emma has placed her stencil on top of the length of cloth to make sure it fits (Figure TJ). Place the screen on top so that there are no gaps. Put out a layer of ink on one side of the screen and (with somebody holding the screen firmly in place) pull the ink from one side of the screen to the other using the squeegee. The squeegee needs to be pulled firmly at an angle of approximately 45 degrees. Repeat this at least twice to ensure all the surface is covered, then carefully lift the screen. If the stencil has worked well on the paper you can move on to print onto cloth (Figure TK).

TK

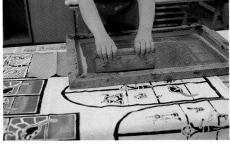

Printing posters

If you are printing onto paper it is useful to have a baseboard that the screen can be attached to with a hinge. This will enable registration marks to be made on the base so that the paper can be placed into the correct position each time a colour is added.

Printing textiles

If you are printing a length of cloth some device must be made to allow for registration. The simplest method is to have a line that can be used to link each print together. Here a drawing of a geranium (Figure TL) was altered slightly so the top of the stem is the same distance away from the edge of the paper as the bottom. The child had only to line up the stems each time to produce a continuous print for a length of cloth (Figure TM).

TL

TM

When printing a length of cloth, two children need to work together, one holding and lining up the screen while the other pulls the colour through. Each print needs to be protected with a paper towel or absorbent paper when the screen is being lined up. This is to prevent the wet ink from being smudged. Allow the print to dry for several hours before moving it.

One of the greatest pleasures is for a child to realise her or his design by printing a length of cloth. It would be very expensive indeed to provide lengths of fabric for all the children who require them. I find jumble sales, auctions and house clearances to be an excellent source of white sheets and use these for any children who cannot provide their own sheet from home.

STRETCHING PAPER FOR PAINTING

If cartridge paper is stretched onto a drawing board, before painting it, this will give the children a good surface to work on and prevent any buckling that may take place when it becomes wet.

1 Place the drawing board into the sink and wash it to make sure there are no traces of old paint.

2 Take a sheet of good cartridge paper and lay it on top of the wet board. It works best if the board has a layer of water on top of it when you place the paper down. Smooth the paper onto the board squashing out surplus water with your hands. Let the top of the paper become thoroughly wet and smooth the paper until it is flat.

TN

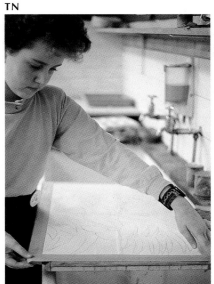

3 Wet 'gum strip' and use it to glue the paper evenly to the board. The gum strip must cover the paper by at least one centimetre all the way around the board (Figure TN).

4 Allow the board to dry in an upright position away from direct heat. It can be painted on directly for a wet-on-wet result, but children usually prefer the control they have over a dry surface. It will take approximately four hours to dry.

I usually mount pictures after children have drawn on the paper. The water will not wash off the drawing, but it does fade it slightly.

MANAGING CLAY

If you are setting up a ceramic work area in school, you should contact your Health and Safety officer and be familiar with the current regulations from COSH.

Storage

Clay is delivered in 25kg bags. It is heavy to transport and so you will want to store it as near to your workroom as possible. Although it is wrapped in polythene, it needs to be stored away from direct heat to prevent it from drying out.

Type of clay

A good all-purpose clay for school use is St. Thomas's Body. This clay is very plastic and is tolerant to misuse. It is possible to use it with stoneware or earthenware glazes.

It is also desirable to have a small amount of red earthenware clay to use with a white slip and transparent glaze for sgraffito techniques.

Glaze

I would suggest keeping six good stoneware glazes bought ready-to-mix from a reputable supplier. In addition, it is useful to have a transparent earthenware glaze to use on red clay.

Glazes need to be mixed with water taking care not to inhale the dust. (Masks are available for this.) They should be stored in lidded buckets and clearly labelled. Schools must not use any glazes that contain lead.

Tools

Wooden rolling pins, knives and a few boxwood tools are all that is required to get started. An 8 x 4-sheet of hardboard cut into squares will provide a work surface that will last a good many years.

Storing work

It is essential that work can be safely stored between lessons. Ideally, you need a 'walk-in store' with shelves that can be clearly labelled for each class. It is important that children wrap their work in polythene to keep it damp and that they write their names on the outside of their bag so they can find it easily.

Clay that is drying out needs to be kept in the kiln room away from the working area. Dust must be kept to a minimum.

Firing

Most kilns operating in schools today have a computerised control box, so a lot of the heartache has been taken out of firing. However, it is important to make sure that all work is thoroughly dried before biscuit-firing. We usually fire the biscuit kiln very slowly to 950°C, the earthenware to 1060°C and the stoneware to 1240 C, with a twenty-minute soak. However, all kilns are different.

Preparation

Have all the tools and clay (divided into the appropriate sized lumps) ready before the class arrives.

Get the children to cover the tables with newspaper before they start. They should wear aprons, preferably the plastic easy-wipe type. Clearing up is then simply a matter of rolling up the paper carefully so that clay does not go on the floor, and brushing up any crumbs that come out of the paper. It should not entail a massive operation of scrubbing tables down. However, the children cannot work on the paper because it will stick to the clay. They need to be given wooden boards or sheets of canvas to work on and these will need to be washed at the end of the lesson.

Allow plenty of time to clear up at the end of the lesson. It is always good to have a quiet time at the end when you can give out homework and review children's achievements rather than having a frantic rush.

Any clay that has been discarded will need to be collected and soaked in bins ready to be reconstituted again. We keep a number of plaster bats in our storage room that are used to dry out clay ready for re-use.

MOULD MAKING

It is not necessary to have specially-prepared moulds to form clay. It is possible to use any absorbent surface. The simplest mould of all is crushed newspaper used to support the clay while it is drying. Even plastic or china plates and bowls may be used if they are lined with an absorbent material such as a paper towel (Figure TO).

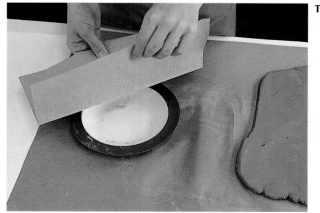

TO

A square of cloth suspended from a frame (e.g. the legs of an upturned stool) can turn a clay tile into a shallow dish. If you decide to make moulds, the best ones are those made using Plaster of Paris.

Again there is a quick and simple way of making these. The plaster needs to set around a negative former. A round object, such as a rubber ball, may be used to make a bowl shape by being pushed up to its middle into a cardboard box full of setting plaster. But if you have time to do things properly, you should make a clay former. The potter's wheel is ideal for making a symmetrical shape. This should be placed on a wooden base and encased in a wooden frame that can hold the plaster. The wood needs to be oiled to prevent the plaster from sticking. Use soft clay around the edges of the frame to prevent plaster from seeping out. Mix the plaster in the proportion of one and a half pounds of plaster to one pint of water, and as it thickens, pour it into the mould. After two or three hours it is safe to remove the clay, but the plaster will not be absorbent enough to use as a mould for at least a week.

Alternatively, it is possible to make a mould on the wheel. To do this, it is necessary to centre a fairly large amount of clay and hollow out the centre to form the negative of the shape required. Once this is done, it needs to be thoroughly dried and fired very slowly during the biscuit phase to avoid cracking. It is then used in its porous biscuit state.

PRESS-MOULDED DISHES

A number of the projects in this book require the use of press-moulded dishes. I have suggested these because they are very easy to use and enable all children to achieve a good result.

TP

Give the children guides to roll their clay between so that they can achieve an even thickness. They need to turn the clay over while they are rolling to prevent it sticking. Any air bubbles that appear should be burst with a knife (Figure TP).

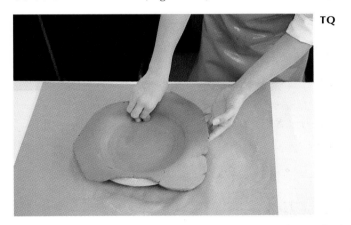

TQ

When the appropriate thickness has been achieved, the clay needs to be carefully laid into the mould and sponged to take up its shape (Figure TQ). A knife or boxwood tool is used to cut an even edge. Do not use a knife with a plaster mould (Figure TR).

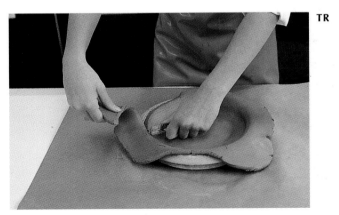

TR

If they are working on a sgraffito technique, the slip should be applied now. Red earthenware clay needs to be coated with white slip. St Thomas's Body needs a reactive slip. The reactive slip may be purchased from Potclays but you can make your own white slip using Lesley's recipe.

Lesley's white earthenware slip

3 parts black ball clay
1 part china clay
Half part-dried red clay (i.e. the clay body)

This works well under a transparent glaze. If you decide on the reactive slip, use it in conjunction with matt dolomite stoneware glaze.

These need to be allowed to dry until they are leather-hard. At this stage the clay will have taken up the shape of the mould, but is still damp. DO NOT ALLOW THE CLAY TO BECOME TOO DRY. When the dishes are leather-hard, prevent them from drying further by wrapping them in polythene. If the slip coating is a little thin, it may be advisable to give them a second coat.

SGRAFFITO

TS

This is simply the scratching away of a surface covering to reveal the body underneath. It is important to plan the design so that it fills the shape well. A pencil may be used to draw out the initial lines, then a boxwood tool may be used to scrape away larger areas. Remember it is important to keep a balance between the two coloured clays (Figure TS).

CREATIVE MOULDING

The moulded shape is very versatile. Two moulded shapes can be joined together and used as the basis of a sculptural form (Figure TT).

TT

When joining two moulds together the clay needs to be in a leather-hard condition. Both surfaces should be scored with a knife to roughen them and then painted with liquid clay to glue them together. The join needs to be worked together on the outside so that the two clays combine. It is necessary to make at least a small hole in shapes that have been joined in this way to allow steam to escape during firing.

GLAZING

A glaze is a special sort of glass with a low thermal expansion and a high alumina content. All glazes contain a mixture of oxides and minerals which need to be mixed with water. A school would be well advised to buy half a dozen good glazes from a reputable supplier and work with those.

When mixing the glaze, carefully empty the contents of the packet into a bucket of water (do this outside wearing a mask) and allow it to soak for an hour or so before sieving. The soaked mixture can then be brushed through the appropriate 'lawn' (special sieve). A mesh of 100 will be suitable for both stoneware and earthenware glazes.

The thickness of the glaze is very important. Too thick and it will peel, crawl or craze, too thin and it will fail to develop. It is useful to make glaze tests before using them with a class. This will enable you to discover their optimum working strengths and allow you to show the children how they should look if applied properly. Generally glaze works well if it has the texture of milk. It should give biscuit-ware a fine covering when placed into the mixture for a few seconds.

The way glaze is applied depends on the finish that is required. If a smooth, even colour is required to finish a pot or tile, the quickest, easiest method is simply to immerse it into the bucket with a quick sweep of the hand. Try to hold it so that as few fingers as possible are in contact with the pot, and lay it down quickly

TU

before the glaze dries. If the finger marks can be filled in with glaze before it dries, they should not show (Figure TU).

If a model is being glazed and several different colours are required, it is better to paint the glaze on. I usually organise it so that the children are working in four groups and each group has access to clearly-labelled pots containing the six

TV

basic colours. Before allowing the children to use the glaze, make sure they understand the need to be careful with the mixture and to mop up any spills as they occur. It is advisable to work on newspaper (Figure TV).

When the glazing is finished, all traces of glaze must be removed from the base of the work by rubbing it off with a damp sponge. This is essential because if any glaze remains on the

base, or melts down from the sides, the work will stick to the kiln during firing.

Un-fired glazed ware must be stored in the kiln room until it is fired.

WORKING WITH CLAY

SLABS

There are a number of products available on the market today that do not require firing. These 'new clays' have only to be left to dry and they will change into a durable material that can withstand the passage of time. All conventional clays require subjection to extreme heat in order for them to become durable and this exposure to extreme heat has to be considered when working with the material. One important factor is the thickness of the walls. A solid lump of clay will dry unevenly in the kiln, and as its particles expand and shrink is likely to fall apart.

It is therefore necessary to adopt methods of working that facilitate even drying. An excellent method of building is that of working with clay rolled out into thin sheets or slabs.

TW

If the slabs are used while the clay is still very wet, it is easy to join it together. Wet clay only needs a little effort in smoothing edges together to enable it to join. This can usefully be applied in projects such as building shoes and modelling clothes for figures.

If, however, you are working on shapes that require firm walls (slab pots or model buildings) then the clay needs to be allowed to dry to become leather-hard before it is joined. The two edges that are to be joined need to be scored with a knife and then painted with slip (liquid clay made from the clay body) to act as a glue. Then they need to have a thin coil of soft clay worked into the join to hold it firm and the whole thing needs to be allowed to dry slowly. If the walls need to be even in thickness, the simplest way of achieving this is to roll the clay out between guides.

The rate at which the clay dries can be controlled by the use of polythene. If soft clay is wrapped in an air-tight polythene bag and stored away from direct heat, it will stay moist almost indefinitely. If a model has been constructed with fine, thin projections, it is advisable to cover them in polythene to slow down the rate at which they can dry until the rest of the model is partly dry. This will prevent uneven drying which often causes delicate structures to crack.

THUMB POTS

The simplest method of working with the clay is to form a thumb pot. Here a ball of clay is gradually hollowed out by pressing your thumb into the centre and squeezing out to thin down the walls. Once the walls are half an inch thick, it can be modelled into a whole range of forms. It is very useful to join two thumb pots together and roll them on the table to produce a perfect egg shape. This can now be the middle of an elephant or the beginning of a seed pod pot. It is important, however, that a small hole is made in any hollow form to allow steam to escape during firing. (See Figure TX.)

TX

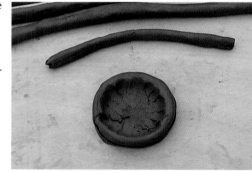

COIL POTS

Another way of building with clay is to build the walls up with strips of clay that are joined together while still soft.

The base is made first by cutting a shape out of a clay slab. Then a number of clay 'sausages' are rolled with the fingers and one by one they are joined onto the base. It is easier to control the shape of your pot if you make a complete ring for each layer and join them on one at a time. Children get on very much better if they use fairly thick coils. Always join downwards, smoothing the clay from the most recent coil to the ones underneath. Joining on the outside first and then on the inside prevents the natural tendency for the form to widen too much … if it widens too much it can collapse! (See Figure TY.)

TY

Coiling can give great freedom in constructing large, asymmetrical forms. The torso (Figure TZ) was made with a coiling technique.

TZ

P ART 4
A SSESSMENT

ASSESSMENT

It is a mistake to think of assessment as something that is done just at the end of a unit of work. All the way through, as the children are developing their ideas, the teacher and the children together are evaluating how things are going. The National Curriculum (August 1991) states: 'Assessment is an integral part of learning and teaching ... pupils involved in art, craft and design are constantly assessing, evaluating and making judgements about their work' (p.49).

It is an on-going process: the teacher and other children offer advice while the work is in progress and the child modifies his or her approach accordingly. Indeed, learning to make critical judgements is part of the artistic process. To tell a child what he should have done at the end of a unit of work may justifiably elicit the response, 'Why didn't you tell me before?' Formative assessment is part and parcel of creation and of the dynamic relationship between teacher and pupil.

However, when the work has been completed, it is necessary to examine what has been achieved and to keep a record of that achievement - the summative assessment.

By far the best record of a child's achievement is his or her sketch book. The fact that the National Curriculum requires the keeping of such a book is excellent. Now all children will have a place to experiment, explore and keep a record of their development. The sketch book enables the teacher to see at a glance the progress that has been made, but this is not an assessment which is readily accessible to the outsider.

Keeping a record of the levels of attainment achieved during the course is more difficult, but an essential feature, not only of the National Curriculum but of the formative and summative assessments. For this reason, I have devised and will - without doubt - revise, an assessment sheet to be completed by the child and the teacher at the end of each unit of work.

The sheet helps the child to identify those aspects of work that are important and enables him or her to make judgements on his or her progress. The teacher is able to comment on the child's self assessment and can use that to help form the statements on the levels of attainment. In addition, at the end of a year or of a Key Stage, there is a record of all that has been achieved with comments on the process.

ART AND DESIGN
PUPIL/TEACHER ASSESSMENT SHEET

NAME: _____ FORM: _____

PROJECT TITLE _____ DATE: _____

TITLE OF WORK (if any) _____ TEACHER: _____

1 Have you **used imaginatively**, i.e. adapted for your own purposes, some of the methods and approaches used by the **artists**, **craftworkers** and **designers** whose work you have studied? Name the people below if you have:

_____

_____

_____

_____

Have **you** used: colour, line, tone, texture, shape, form, pattern? Comment below.

_____

_____

_____

_____

2 Have you experimented with a range of **media**, **tools** and **techniques**? **If so, circle the ones you have used, add any which are not mentioned.**

MEDIA: batik, charcoal, clay, coloured pencils, dry pastel, felt-tip, ink, oil pastel, pencil, photographs, plaster, PVA, water colour.
TOOLS: brushes, enlargers, modelling tools, paint brushes, pens, printing frames, potters' wheel, scissors, tjantings.
TECHNIQUES: collage, constructing, cross-hatching, drawing, modelling, painting, printing, shading.

3 While you were working on this project, did you alter your approach after discussion with anyone, e.g. teacher or other pupils? If so, briefly try to describe your change.

_____

_____

_____

_____

4 How have you shown development in your chosen idea or theme?

_____

_____

_____

_____

5 If you were to do this work again, what would you do differently?

_____

_____

_____

_____

Signed (Pupil): _____

Teacher comment: _____

_____

_____

ATTAINMENT TARGET 1: _____

ATTAINMENT TARGET 2: _____

LINKS TO EXPRESSIVE ARTS CURRICULUM IN SCOTLAND
levels D and E

(Correct at the time of going to press.
See also page 95.)

Outcomes	Strands	Attainment Targets	Schemes of Work
USING MATERIALS TECHNIQUES SKILLS AND MEDIA	1 USING MEDIA	**D1** Use a range of media, in painting, printing, modelling, 3-D construction or fabric-related activities, showing some understanding of the qualities of these and evidence of personal choice.	Self Portrait: sessions 4 and 5; Masks: sessions 3 to 5; The Local Environment : sessions 1 to 6; A Room with a View: sessions 3 and 4; Plant Studies: sessions 2, 4 to 6; Plant Studies – Printing: sessions 1 and 5; Shoe Studies: sessions 3 to 5 ,7 to 10; Animal Studies: Clay, Card, Plaster and Batik; Conservation of the Environment: sessions 3 and 4; Light: sessions 1 to 6; Reflections: sessions 2 and 3; Water: sessions 2 and 5; Hands: sessions 2 to 4; Portrait Heads: sessions 3 to 5; Figure Modelling: sessions 2 and 3; Still Life: sessions 2 to 5; A Gothic Church: sessions 2 and 3; Fastenings: sessions 1 and 2; Natural Forms: sessions 1 to 4; A Gallery Visit: sessions 1,2,4 and 5
	2 USING VISUAL ELEMENTS	**D2** Use with some guidance and show progressive understanding of the visual elements through making images and objects.	Self Portrait: sessions 3 to 5; Masks: session 2; The Local Environment: sessions 3 and 4; A Room with a View: sessions 3 and 4; Plant Studies: session 2; Shoe Studies: session 2; Animal Studies: session 2; Conservation of the Environment: session 2; Light: sessions 1 to 6; Reflections: sessions 1 to 3; Water: sessions 3 and 4; Hands: sessions 2 and 3; Still Life: sessions 3 and 4; Changed Viewpoint: session 4; A Gothic Church: session 3; Fastenings: session 2; Metamorphosis: sessions 3 and 4; Natural Forms: sessions 2 and 4; A Gallery Visit: sessions 1 and 5
	3 OBSERVING AND RECORDING	**D3** Use a limited number of ways of recording e.g. photography, computer draw and paint programmes, annotating sketches. Use these studies for other work.	Self Portrait: sessions 1 and 2; Masks: sessions 1 and 2; The Local Environment: session 1, Homeworks 2 and 3; A Room with a View: session 1, Homework 1; Plant Studies: session 1; Shoe Studies: session 1; Animal Studies (8 to 13): session 1; Conservation of the Environment: session 1; Light: sessions 1 to 3; Water: session 2; Hands: session 1; Portrait Heads: session 1; Still Life: session 1; A Gothic Church: session 2; Fastenings: sessions 1 and 2; Metamorphosis: sessions 1 and 2; Natural Forms (26,27 and 28); session 1; A Gallery Visit: sessions 1,2 and 4
EXPRESSING IDEAS THOUGHTS SOLUTIONS AND FEELINGS	4 EXPRESSING FEELINGS AND IDEAS	**D4** Show an increased interest in representing what is seen. Use a range of visual devices to attempt realism e.g. in perspective, in realistic colour, in detail and in pattern.	Self Portrait: sessions 3 to 6; Masks: session 2; A Room with a View: session 2; Shoe Studies: sessions 2,9 and 10; Animal Studies: session 2; Conservation of the Environment: sessions 2 to 4; Light: session 7; Hands: session 8; Changed Viewpoint: sessions 2 and 3; Fastenings: session 2; Natural Forms: sessions 2 to 4; A Gallery Visit: session 5
		E1 Consider, select and use appropriately a range of media occasionally combining some of these. Work confidently in a range of process-based activities.	
		E2 Show understanding of the visual elements, and use these in making images and objects. Demonstrate through discussion and application the relationship between at least two of these e.g. colour and tone.	
		E3 Use a variety of ways of recording e.g. drawing, painting, sketching, still or video photography. Use these as the basis for further development in a variety of media.	
		E4 Use a range of visual methods when expressing feelings and ideas, by attempting perspective, realistic colour and tone. Use abstraction to express fantasy and imagination, occasionally using images from the mass media.	

Outcomes	Strands	Attainment Targets	Schemes of Work
	5 DESIGNING	**D5** Within a given brief investigate possible solutions by making some sketches, notes or by collecting visual material. Suggest by drawing, visual presentation or discussion, at least one possible solution to a design problem.	**E5** With some independence, within a given brief, investigate by making some sketches, notes or gathering other evidence. Communicate or produce possible design solutions in graphic or other form in which one or two ideas are presented clearly and attractively.	Self Portrait: session 3; Masks: session 2; The Local Environment: sessions 3 and 4; A Room with a View: session 2; Plant Studies: sessions 3 and 4; Shoe Studies: sessions 2 and 7; Animal Studies (8 to 13): session 2; Conservation of the Environment: session 2; Light: session 7; Reflections: session 3; Still Life: sessions 4 and 6; Changed Viewpoint: sessions 2 and 4; Fastenings: session 2; Metamorphosis: sessions 3 and 4; Natural Forms: session 2; A Gallery Visit: session 5
EVALUATING AND APPRECIATING	**6** USING INFORMATION AND RESPONDING		**E6** Find out about an artist or designer and his/her work by collating materials and information from several sources. e.g. art reference books, postcards or computer data-base. Make one or two personal statements about their own and an artist or designer's work, showing an understanding of the use of the visual elements to support an opinion. Evaluate their own design work, showing understanding of a design process, indicating modifications where appropriate.	Self Portrait: sessions 1,4 and 6; Masks: sessions 1,2 and 5; The Local Environment: session 1; A Room with a View: sessions 1 and 2; Plant Studies: sessions 1 and 3; Animal Studies (8): session 2; Animal Studies (9 to 13): session 1; Conservation of the Environment: session 2; Light: session 1; Reflections: session 3; Water: sessions 1 and 2; Hands: session 2; Figure Modelling: session 1; Still Life: session 4; Changed Viewpoint: session 1; A Gothic Church: sessions 1 and 2; Fastenings: session 2; Metamorphosis: session 1; Natural Forms: (26 to 28): session 1; A Gallery Visit: sessions 1 to 4

91

LINKS TO ART IN THE NATIONAL CURRICULUM ENGLAND AND WALES

(Correct at the time of going to press. See also page 95.)

KEY STAGE 3 ATTAINMENT TARGET 1: INVESTIGATING AND MAKING

END OF KEY STAGE STATEMENTS

By the end of Key Stage 3, pupils should have demonstrated that they can:

use expressive and technical skill to analyse and present, in visual form, what they observe, remember and imagine.

develop and sustain a chosen idea or theme in their work, investigating and explaining their use of a range of visual and other sources.

PROGRAMMES OF STUDY

Pupils should:

1 develop skills for analysing and recording from observation, memory and imagination, using a variety of media.

2 keep a sketch book to collect and record information and ideas for independent work.

3 select and organise a range of source material to stimulate and develop ideas or themes.

4 discuss the impact of source material on the development of their work.

5 select from the range of visual elements and interpret their use in making images and artifacts.

---

1 Self Portrait: sessions 1 and 2; Masks: sessions 1 and 2; The Local Environment: sessions 1 and 2; A Room with a View: sessions 1 and 2; Plant Studies: sessions 1 and 2; Plant Studies – Printing: sessions 1 and 2; Shoe Studies: sessions 1,2 and 6; Animal Studies – Modelling: session 1, Construction: session 1, Batik: session 1, Pottery: session 1, Plaster Tiles: session 1, Decorated Dishes: session 1; Conservation of the Environment: session 1; Light: sessions 1 to 6; Reflections: sessions 1 and 2; Water: sessions 1 and 2; Hands: session 1; Portrait Heads: session 1; Still Life: sessions 1 to 3; Changed Viewpoint: session 1; A Gothic Church: sessions 2 and 3; Fastenings: sessions 1 and 2; Metamorphosis: sessions 1 and 2; Natural Forms – Printing: session 1; Natural Forms – Ceramics: session 1; Natural Forms – Painting: sessions 1 to 4; A Gallery Visit: sessions 1,2 and 4

2 Self Portrait: sessions 1 to 3; Masks: sessions 1 and 2; The Local Environment: sessions 1 to 3; A Room with a View: sessions 1 and 2; Plant Studies: sessions 1 to 5; Plant Studies – Printing: session 1; Shoe Studies: sessions 1 to 3; Animal Studies – Modelling: sessions 1 and 2, Construction: session 1, Batik: sessions 1 and 2, Pottery: sessions 1 and 2, Plaster Tiles: sessions 1 and 2, Decorated Dishes: session 1; Conservation of the Environment: sessions 1 and 2; Light: sessions 1 to 4; Reflections: sessions 1 and 2; Water: sessions 1 to 3; Hands: sessions 1 and 2; Portrait Heads: sessions 1 and 3; Figure Modelling: session 1; Still Life: sessions 1,2,4, and 5; Changed Viewpoint: session 1; A Gothic Church: session 2; Fastenings: session 1; Metamorphosis: session 1; Natural Forms – Printing: session 1; Natural Forms – Ceramics: session 1; Natural Forms – Painting: session 1; A Gallery Visit: sessions 1,2 and 4

3 Self Portrait: sessions 2 and 3; Masks: sessions 2 and 3; The Local Environment: sessions 2, 4 and 5; A Room with a View: session 2; Plant Studies: session 3; Plant Studies – Printing: session 3; Shoe Studies: sessions 2 and 9; Animal Studies – Modelling: session 2, Construction: session 2, Batik: session 2, Pottery: session 2, Plaster Tiles: session 2, Decorated Dishes: session 2; Conservation of the Environment: session 2; Light: session 7; Reflections: session 3; Water: session 3; Hands: session 1; Portrait Heads: session 1; Still Life: sessions 4 and 6; Changed Viewpoint: sessions 2 and 4; A Gothic Church: session 3; Fastenings: session 2; Metamorphosis: sessions 2 and 3; Natural Forms – Painting: session 2; A Gallery Visit: session 5

4 Self Portrait: sessions 3 and 6; Masks: sessions 3 and 5; The Local Environment: sessions 4 to 6; A Room with a View: session 2; Plant Studies: sessions 2,3 and 6; Plant Studies – Printing: sessions 3 and 5; Shoe Studies: sessions 2, 5 and 10; Animal Studies – Modelling: session 4, Construction: session 4, Batik: session 4, Pottery: session 4, Plaster Tiles: session 3, Decorated Dishes: session 4; Conservation of the Environment: sessions 2 and 3; Light: session 7; Reflections: session 3; Water: sessions 4 and 5; Hands: session 4; Portrait Heads: session 3; Figure Modelling: session 5; Still Life: sessions 5 and 8; Changed Viewpoint: session 4; A Gothic Church: session 3; Fastenings: session 2; Metamorphosis: sessions 3 and 4; Natural Forms – Printing: sessions 3 and 5; Natural Forms – Painting: sessions 2 and 4; A Gallery Visit: session 5

5 Self Portrait; Masks; The Local Environment; A Room with a View; Plant Studies; Plant Studies – Printing; Shoe Studies; Animal Studies – Modelling, Construction, Batik, Pottery, Plaster Tiles, Decorated Dishes; Conservation of the Environment; Light; Reflections; Water; Hands; Portrait Heads; Figure Modelling; Still Life; Changed Viewpoint; A Gothic Church; Fastenings; Metamorphosis; Natural Forms – Printing; Natural Forms – Ceramics; Natural Forms – Painting; A Gallery Visit

End of Key Stage Statements	Programmes of Study	Schemes of Work
apply a broad understanding of the elements of art and design and the characteristics of materials, tools and techniques to implement their ideas.	6 use a wide range of visual elements and interpret their use in making images and artefacts.	6 Self Portrait: session 3; Masks: session 2; The Local Environment: sessions 1 and 4; A Room with a View: session 2; Plant Studies: session 3; Plant Studies – Printing: session 3; Shoe Studies: sessions 2 and 7; Animal Studies – Modelling: session 2, Construction: session 2, Pottery: session 2, Plaster Tiles: session 2, Decorated Dishes: session 2; Conservation of the Environment: sessions 3 and 4; Light: sessions 1 to 7; Reflections: sessions 1 to 3; Water: sessions 2, 4 and 5; Hands: session 2; Portrait Heads: session 3; Figure Modelling: session 2; Still Life: sessions 4 and 5; Changed Viewpoint: sessions 2 to 4; A Gothic Church: sessions 2 and 3; Fastenings: session 2; Metamorphosis: sessions 3 and 4; Natural Forms – Printing: sessions 2 and 3; Natural Forms – Ceramics: session 2; Natural Forms – Painting: sessions 1 to 4; A Gallery Visit: session 5
explore and experiment with materials, images and ideas for three dimensional work, and realise their intentions.	7 explore and experiment with materials, images and ideas for three dimensional work, and realise their intentions.	7 Masks; The Local Environment; A Room with a View: session 4; Plant Studies; Shoe Studies: sessions 6 to 10; Animal Studies – Modelling, Construction, Pottery, Plaster Tiles, Decorated Dishes; Conservation of the Environment: sessions 3 and 4; Water: sessions 4 and 5; Hands; Portrait Heads; Figure Modelling; Still Life: sessions 1 and 2; A Gothic Church: session 3; Fastenings: session 3; Metamorphosis: sessions 3 and 4; Natural Forms – Ceramics: sessions 1 and 2; A Gallery Visit: session 5
modify their work as it progresses, reviewing its meaning and explaining the reasons for change.	8 modify and refine their work as the result of continuing and informed discussion.	8 Self Portrait: sessions 4 and 5; Masks: sessions 3 and 4; The Local Environment: sessions 4 to 6; A Room with a View: sessions 3 and 4; Plant Studies: sessions 2 to 5; Plant Studies – Printing: sessions 3 and 4; Shoe Studies: sessions 3 to 5, 9 and 10; Animal Studies – Modelling: sessions 2 and 3, Construction: sessions 2 to 4, Batik: sessions 2 and 3, Pottery: sessions 2 and 3, Plaster Tiles: session 2, Decorated Dishes: sessions 2 and 3; Conservation of the Environment: sessions 3 and 4; Light: session 7; Reflections: session 3; Water: sessions 4 and 5; Hands: sessions 2 and 3; Portrait Heads: sessions 3 and 4; Figure Modelling: sessions 2 and 3; Still Life: sessions 2 to 6; Changed Viewpoint: sessions 2 to 4; A Gothic Church: session 3; Fastenings: session 2; Metamorphosis: sessions 3 and 4; Natural Forms – Printing: sessions 2 and 3; Natural Forms – Ceramics: session 2; Natural Forms – Painting: sessions 2 to 4; A Gallery Visit: session 5
discuss their work using a developing, specialist vocabulary.	9 discuss their work using a developing, specialist vocabulary.	9 Self Portrait; Masks; The Local Environment; A Room with a View; Plant Studies; Plant Studies – Printing; Shoe Studies; Animal Studies – Modelling, Construction, Batik, Pottery, Plaster Tiles, Decorated Dishes; Conservation of the Environment; Light; Reflections; Water; Hands; Portrait Heads; Figure Modelling; Still Life; Changed Viewpoint; A Gothic Church; Fastenings; Metamorphosis; Natural Forms – Printing; Natural Forms – Ceramics: Natural Forms – Painting; A Gallery Visit
plan and make further developments in response to their own and others evaluations.	10 plan and make further developments in response to their own and others evaluations.	10 Self Portrait: session 6; Masks: session 5; The Local Environment: session 4; Shoe Studies: session 1; Conservation of the Environment: sessions 3 and 4; Water: session 5; Hands: session 4; Portrait Heads: session 3; Figure Modelling: session 2; Still Life: session 6; Changed Viewpoint: session 4; A Gothic Church: session 3; Fastenings: session 2; Metamorphosis: session 2; Natural Forms – Printing: session 3; Natural Forms – Ceramics: session 2; Natural Forms – Painting: session 3; A Gallery Visit: session 5

KEY STAGE 3 ATTAINMENT TARGET 2: KNOWLEDGE AND UNDERSTANDING

END OF KEY STAGE STATEMENTS	PROGRAMMES OF STUDY	SCHEMES OF WORK
By the end of Key Stage 3 pupils should have demonstrated that they can:	Pupils should:	
evaluate the work of artists, recognising that images, symbols and objects are influenced by diverse cultural and social conventions.	1 recognise the diverse ways that artists working in different cultures view and represent the world.	**1** Self Portrait: session 1; Masks: session 1; The Local Environment: session 1; A Room with a View: session 1; Plant Studies: session 2; Plant Studies – Printing: session 3; Shoe Studies: session 2; Animal Studies – Modelling: session 1, Construction: session 1, Batik: session 1, Pottery: session 1, Plaster Tiles: session 1, Decorated Dishes: session 1; Conservation of the Environment: session 2; Light: session 1; Reflections: session 3; Water: session 1; Hands: session 1; Portrait Heads: session 1; Figure Modelling: session 1; Still Life: session 4; Changed Viewpoint: session 1; A Gothic Church: sessions 1 and 2; Fastenings: session 2; Metamorphosis: session 1; Natural Forms – Printing: session 1; Natural Forms – Ceramics: session 1; Natural Forms – Painting: session 1; A Gallery Visit: sessions 1 to 5
understand the principal features of our artistic heritage and appreciate a variety of other artistic traditions.	2 analyse the work of other artists and understand the main codes and conventions they use to convey meaning.	**2** Self Portrait: session 1; Masks: session 1; The Local Environment: session 1; A Room with a View: session 1; Plant Studies: session 2; Plant Studies – Printing: session 3; Shoe Studies: session 2; Animal Studies – Modelling: session 1, Construction: session 1, Batik: session 1, Pottery: session 1, Plaster Tiles: session 1, Decorated Dishes: session 1; Conservation of the Environment: session 2; Light: session 1; Reflections: session 3; Water: session 1; Hands: session 2; Portrait Heads: session 1; Figure Modelling: session 1; Still Life: session 4; Changed Viewpoint: session 1; A Gothic Church: sessions 1 and 2; Fastenings: session 2; Metamorphosis: session 1; Natural Forms – Printing: session 1; Natural Forms – Ceramics: session 1; Natural Forms – Painting: session 1; A Gallery Visit: sessions 1 to 5
understand how methods and approaches of other artists can be used imaginatively in the presentation of their own ideas and feelings.	3 understand the distinctive characteristics of art from the following periods – medieval, baroque, classical, romantic, post-impressionism, expressionism, cubism, surrealism, abstract expressionism – recognising the broad relationships between them.	**3** Self Portrait: session 1; A Room with a View: session 1; Plant Studies: session 2; Shoe Studies: session 2; Animal Studies – Modelling: session 1, Construction: session 1, Conservation of the Environment: session 2; Light: session 1; Reflections: session 3; Water: sessions 1 and 2; Hands: session 2; Portrait Heads: session 1; Figure Modelling: session 1; A Gothic Church: sessions 1 and 2; Fastenings: session 1; Still Life: session 4; Changed Viewpoint: session 1; A Gallery Visit: sessions 1 to 5; Natural Forms – Painting: session 1; Metamorphosis: session 2;
	4 analyse the work of significant artists and understand the contribution each has made to the development of artistic achievement.	**4** Self Portrait: session 1; A Room with a View: session 1; Plant Studies: session 2; Shoe Studies: session 2; Animal Studies – Modelling: session 1, Construction: session 1, Conservation of the Environment: session 2; Light: session 1; Reflections: session 3; Water: session 1; Hands: session 2; Portrait Heads: session 1; Figure Modelling: session 1; A Gothic Church: session 3; Fastenings: session 2; Metamorphosis: session 1; Natural Forms – Painting: session 1; A Gallery Visit: sessions 1 to 4
	5 express opinions and justify preferences about art, having respect for the views of others, using a developing specialist vocabulary.	**5** Self Portrait: session 1; Masks: session 2; The Local Environment: session 1; A Room with a View: session 1; Plant Studies: session 2; Plant Studies – Printing: session 3; Shoe Studies: session 2; Animal Studies – Modelling: session 1, Construction: session 1, Batik: session 1, Pottery: session 1, Plaster Tiles: session 1; Decorated Dishes: session 3; Light: session 1; Reflections: session 3; Water: session 1; Hands: session 1; Conservation of the Environment: sessions 2 and 3; Portrait Heads: session 1; Figure Modelling: session 1; Still Life: session 4; Changed Viewpoint: session 1; A Gothic Church: session 1; Fastenings: session 2; Metamorphosis: session 1; Natural Forms – Printing: session 1; Natural Forms – Ceramics: session 1; Natural Forms – Painting: session 1; A Gallery Visit: sessions 1 to 4
	6 use their knowledge of the methods and approaches of artists to enrich their own work.	**6** Self Portrait: session 4; Masks: session 3; The Local Environment: session 4; A Room with a View: sessions 2 to 4; Plant Studies: sessions 2, 3 and 5; Plant Studies – Printing: session 3; Shoe Studies: sessions 3 to 5; Animal Studies – Modelling: sessions 2 and 3; Construction: sessions 2 and 3, Batik: sessions 2 and 3, Pottery: sessions 2 and 3, Plaster Tiles: sessions 2 and 3, Decorated Dishes: sessions 2 and 3; Conservation of the Environment: sessions 3 and 4; Light: session 7; Reflections: session 4; Water: sessions 3 to 5; Hands: sessions 2 and 3; Portrait Heads: sessions 3 and 4; Figure Modelling: sessions 2 and 3; Still Life: sessions 5 to 7; Changed Viewpoint: sessions 2 to 4; A Gothic Church: session 3; Fastenings: session 2; Metamorphosis: sessions 3 and 4; Natural Forms – Printing: sessions 2 to 5; Natural Forms – Ceramics: session 2; Natural Forms – Painting: sessions 2 to 4; A Gallery Visit: sessions 1,2 4, and 5

94

INDEX

✂ -

At the time of going to press the National Curriculum for Art (England and Wales) and the Expressive Arts Curriculum (Scotland) were still in draft form. If you would like to receive updated versions of the tables on pages 90-94 when the curriculums are finalised, please complete and return this form (or a photocopy of it).

Please send me updated tables linking **Programmes of Study in Art & Design** to:

                                     tick as required

National Curriculum for Art (England and Wales)   ☐

Expressive Arts Curriculum (Scotland)   ☐

Name _____

Address _____

_____

_____

_____

Please return to: **Marketing Department, Simon & Schuster Education, Campus 400, Maylands Avenue, Hemel Hempstead HP2 7EZ**